FAMILY PLACEMENT
FOR CHILDREN
IN CARE

PUBLISHED BY
BRITISH AGENCIES FOR
ADOPTION & FOSTERING
11 SOUTHWARK STREET
LONDON SE1 1RQ
© BAAF 1988
ISBN 0 903534 74 6
ISSN 0260 0811
DESIGNED BY ANDREW HAIG
TYPESET BY INTERTYPE LIMITED
PRINTED AND BOUND IN ENGLAND

RESEARCH SERIES: 5

Family placement for children in care

a guide to the literature

◆

Martin Shaw

BRITISH AGENCIES FOR
ADOPTION & FOSTERING

Contents

for Tony Hall
Director of BAAF 1978-1986
with affection and thanks

Introduction

The flow of books and articles on family placement – children in foster and adoptive homes – has reached such a high level since the mid 1970s that it is virtually impossible for the newcomer to know where to begin or even for those who have some familiarity with the literature to keep track of new material. This publication is addressed to three more or less distinct audiences:

a general, non-social-work readership who, as concerned citizens or interested professionals (teachers, doctors, lawyers, journalists and others), are seeking a way into the sometimes complicated world of family placement and are at a loss to know where to start

social workers and social work managers already trained and experienced in child welfare and seeking to refresh or update their knowledge

a more specialised social work audience who have some knowledge at both the 'basic' and more 'advanced' levels, but who are increasingly bemused by the flow of new material and wish to impose some order on their studies. This audience ranges from specialist workers in family placement to students in training who wish to make a special study of family placement.

In the hope of making this source-book easier to use, a starring system has been devised with the above users in mind: general readers may find the double-starred (**) material most approachable as an introduction to the particular topic; single-starred material (*) is recommended to those seeking updating. The presence or absence of stars should not be taken as a judgement on the actual quality of the material. Inevitably, judgements of this kind are to be found in some of the annotations, but ultimately the assessment of an item's worth is the reader's business. Every item included is, in the compiler's view, worthy of someone's attention.

Subject matter
As the title indicates, the subject matter of this publication is the family placement of children in care, that is to say in foster homes or adoptive homes. Because of their relevance to family placement, some references are

included on children in care generally, as well as to those who might be described as on the edge of care. Residential or group care references are not included, nor is the large and growing literature on child abuse and child sexual abuse, except where there is direct reference to family placement.

References are also largely restricted to social work literature, though there are some references to legal and medical material that is linked directly to family placement.

Coverage
A few readers might wish a bibliography to include everything that has ever been written on the subject, and indeed bibliographers sometimes give the impression of seeking to demonstrate that their sources are even more obscure and inaccessible than the previous person's. Most readers, however, will wish for a degree of selectivity, and the following self-imposed rules have been followed to that end:

1 few items published prior to 1970 have been included, on the grounds that the family placement scene has changed so much since then as to make much earlier material irrelevant. Exceptions to this rule are those 'classics' which have continuing relevance
2 references are restricted to material readily available through libraries with access to the Inter-Library Loan Service, and worth the expense involved in seeking it out. One person's obscure journal is another's regular bedtime reading, however, and the compiler would welcome information on any important omissions
3 items included are restricted to material which can fairly be described as 'published', which means that many interesting documents intended primarily for internal circulation within family placement agencies have been omitted. Lest there be any suspicion of bias against 'non-academic' sources, academic theses have also been omitted because of their limited availability to the general reader
4 where a writer has produced a series of articles culminating in a book (eg Maluccio and colleagues on permanency planning), references to the earlier articles have generally been omitted
5 recent years have seen a rapid increase in the amount of material published in audio-cassette or video-cassette rather than in printed format. Material of this kind, which must soon merit a 'bibliography' of its own, has been excluded from the present publication.

Sources

The journal sources used are: *Adolescence, Adoption & Fostering, American Journal of Community Psychology, American Journal of Orthopsychiatry, British Journal of Social Work, *Child Adoption, Child Development, Child Psychiatry & Human Development, Child Psychology & Psychiatry, Child Welfare, Children & Youth Services Review, Community Care, Family Process, Foster Care, International Journal of Social Psychiatry, Journal of Adolescence, Journal of Clinical Child Psychology, Journal of Consulting & Clinical Psychology, Journal of Marriage & the Family, Journal of Social Policy, Journal of Social Service Research, Psychological Bulletin, Psychological Reports, Public Welfare, Smith College Studies in Social Work, Social Casework, Social Service Review, Social Work, Social Work Research & Abstracts* and *Social Work Today.*

Format

As the contents page shows, the items are presented in sequence under various headings, beginning with general material on children in care, and moving on to foster family care and adoption. In organising the material, it was felt that most readers would find it helpful to have items dealing specifically with ethnic issues in a separate section. Each section or subsection is prefaced by a brief commentary which, without embarking upon a wholesale review of the literature, is intended to set the references in context. In both commentary and notes those authors whose work is included in this publication are shown in block capitals. Following normal bibliographical practice, articles are shown in roman and books in italic type.

Acknowledgments

I am indebted to a number of colleagues at the University of Leicester and

---

Child Adoption was the forerunner of *Adoption & Fostering,* published by British Agencies for Adoption & Fostering (BAAF), which has itself experienced several changes of name in the last decade or so in order to allow its title to reflect the organisation's expanding role in UK child welfare. During the period under review it was known first as the Association of British Adoption Agencies, and later as the Association of British Agencies for Fostering and Adoption. Thus, there are items listed here under all three metamorphoses – ABAA, ABAFA and BAAF.

at BAAF for their various contributions which made this publication possible:

the Research Board of the University for a grant towards the financial costs of the project

Stephen Rawlinson and his colleagues in the University Library for their diligence and patience in dealing with my innumerable requests for materials

Dr Judith Masson in the Law Department for help and advice

Sandra Butler in the School of Social Work for her help, suggestions and unfailing moral support

and Prue Chennells of BAAF for her suggestions on additional material, expert editorial guidance and encouragement throughout the project.

Despite so much professional advice, guidance and assistance, what follows will doubtless contain errors, omissions and misjudgements, for which I take full responsibility.

Martin Shaw
University of Leicester
School of Social Work

September 1987

1 Children in care

CHILD WELFARE POLICY AND HISTORY

Anyone coming fresh to the general literature quickly becomes aware of a gap which more experienced readers have come to take for granted – the lack of a comprehensive study of the UK child care/child welfare field. British writers offer the historical survey, the small-scale study, the review of the literature, or a theoretical analysis of one part of the field. US writers offer all of these and the comprehensive, not to say encyclopaedic, handbook of theory and practice designed to meet every need within one volume. It is tempting to try to explain this difference between UK and US writers in terms of national character, but it probably has more to do with the economics of publishing in their respective countries. Whatever the reasons, the UK reader is compelled either to study a range of home-grown publications and attempt a synthesis of their often disparate material, or else to plunge into a US compendium and be left with the none-too-easy task of translation into terms applicable to the UK scene. US writers, with a few laudable exceptions, seem totally unaware of the UK literature, so we cannot even hope for our American cousins to do our homework for us!

Those seeking a way into the literature may find it helpful to start with a good history (PACKMAN or HEYWOOD), and move on to PARKER for the organisational context and an introduction to the main issues, before making selective use of MAIDMAN.

001   **HEYWOOD J (1978) *Children in care* 3rd edition Routledge & Kegan Paul. 272pp.
Historical study of the development of attitudes to and services for children 'deprived of normal home life'.

002   HOLMAN R (1980) *Inequality in child care* 2nd edition Child Poverty Action Group & Family Rights Group. 48pp.
Pamphlet drawing attention to the effects of relative deprivation on families, including those whose children come into care. Argues for less attention to 'rescue' and more to preventive services.

003   KADUSHIN A (1971) 'Child welfare' in H S Maas (ed) *Research in the social services: a five-year review* NY: National Association of Social Workers, 13-69.
Chapter reviewing mainly US research studies 1966-1971, including foster family care and adoption. A 1966 publication in this series by the same editor looks at earlier studies dating back to the 1940s.

004   KADUSHIN A (1977) 'Myths and dilemmas in child welfare' *Child Welfare* 56,3,March, 141-153.
Brief resumé of some unfounded assumptions and such dilemmas as children's rights versus parents' rights, children's needs v rights, stability v innovation.

005   LAIRD J & HARTMAN A (eds) (1985) *A handbook of child welfare: context, knowledge and practice* NY: Collier-Macmillan. 752pp.
A weighty collection in every way – papers by 45 contributors bound together within an ecological framework. Not for beginners but much food for thought for those further on.

006   LAMBERT L & STREATHER J (1980) *Children in changing families* Macmillan. 196pp.
Analysis and discussion of findings from the National Child Development Study on children growing up in care, or in adoptive or one-parent families. (See also 380, 394 and 397.)

007   **MAIDMAN F (ed) (1984) *Child welfare: a source book of knowledge and practice* NY: Child Welfare League of America. 454pp.
Described as a 'one-stop', 'hands-on' volume to which workers at all levels of expertise can turn for the practice wisdom they seek or for references regarding more detailed information. Chapters on an ecological approach to child welfare problems and practice, child protection, community work; child neglect and abuse (including sexual abuse); foster care; residential care; adoption; unmarried parents; and adolescents. Appendices on problem-solving approach and assessment frameworks.

008   MANDELL BR (1973) *Where are the children: a class analysis of foster care & adoption* Massachusetts: Lexington Books. 215pp.
Marxist critique of the US child welfare system. The author argues that a class analysis pinpoints the problems more precisely than does either a purely psychological analysis of individual motivation and personality dynamics or an analysis of role relationships divorced from a view of the larger social system.

009   **PACKMAN J (1981) *The child's generation* 2nd edition. Basil Blackwell & Martin Robertson. 202pp.
Probably the best introduction to the historical development of the child care service, from World War II till around 1980.

010 **PARKER RA (ed) (1980) *Caring for separated children: plans, procedures, and priorities* Macmillan. 190pp.
Report of a National Children's Bureau working party set up "to consider the care, welfare and education of children separated from their families for recurrent or long periods". Given a particular brief to consider means of planning to promote continuity and quality in the children's care. The report considers the legal and administrative framework, causes of concern, prevention, key people and decisions in planning, and new resources and solutions for the future.

011 REINACH E (ed) (1981) *Decision making in child care* Research Highlights no.1, University of Aberdeen Department of Social Work. Scottish Academic Press. 84pp.
Collection of papers on policy issues, including decision making and the implications of research findings for fostering and adoption as placement options.

012 SCHORR AL (ed) (1975) *Children and decent people* Allen & Unwin. 222pp.
The editor and his contributors were concerned to seek out "the reasons why so many children do badly in the United States", but their findings also have relevance to the UK. Of particular interest are the papers by Shirley Jenkins on 'Child welfare as a class system' (pp 3-23) and Martin Rein *et al* on 'Foster family care: myth and reality' (pp 24-52).

013 ZUCKERMAN E (1983) *Child welfare* NY: Free Press/Collier-Macmillan. 218 pp.
Discussion of policy and practice issues in the child welfare field from the stage of intake and preventive work to planning for children in long-term care.

LAW AND ADMINISTRATION

With such rapid changes and developments in legislation and case law, any legal text will be somewhat out of date – and, to that extent, inaccurate – by the day of its publication. With this reservation, HOGGETT and HOGGETT & PEARL in their 1987 editions will make clear and reliable guides. The BAAF journal *Adoption & Fostering* provides regular updating on matters of law.

014 ADCOCK M, WHITE R & ROWLANDS O (1983) *The administrative parent: a study of the assumption of parental rights* BAAF. 92pp.
DHSS-sponsored research study of policies and practices in relation to the assumption of parental rights. (See also 032.)

015   BAAF (1984) *Taking a stand: child psychiatrists in custody, access and disputed adoption cases* BAAF. 84pp.
Seminar papers and discussion group reports on a range of topics including the child psychiatrist in court, the outcome of adoption, assessing fitness to parent, and child abuse.

016   BAAF (1984) *Consent to medical treatment for children in care or placed for adoption* BAAF.

017   BAAF (1984) *A-Z of changes in the law (England and Wales)* BAAF.

018   BAAF 1984) *A-Z of changes in the law in Scotland* BAAF.

019   BAAF (1986) *Custodianship* BAAF.
Practice notes on aspects of child care law and administration.

020   **HOGGETT B (1987) *Parents and children* 3rd edition. Sweet & Maxwell.
Excellent guide to child care legislation and case law.

021   *HOGGETT BM & PEARL DS (1987) *The family, law and society: cases and materials 2nd edition.* Butterworths. 720pp.
As the title suggests, this publication covers much more than the law relating to children in care. Particularly valuable in linking material on law and social work practice.

022   LAMBERT L & ROWE J (1974) 'Children in care and the assumption of parental rights by local authorities' *Child Adoption* 78, 4 of 1974, 13-23.
Small-scale study seeking reasons for the wide variations in the use made by local authorities of powers to assume parental rights over children in care. Differences appeared to relate more to agency policy and practices than to the characteristics of children or families.

023   **MacLEOD SM & GILTINAN D (1987) *Child care law: a summary of the law in Scotland* BAAF. 28pp.
Written for social workers and other interested professionals, this booklet covers private and local authority care, children's hearings, custody and adoption.

024   RAWSTRON D (ed) (1981) *Rights of children* BAAF. 40pp.
Conference papers by Michael Freeman on the rights of children in care; Margaret Adcock on the right to permanent placement; and HK Bevan on rights of children of marital breakdown; with, as an appendix, the proposed visiting code from the *Justice* Report, *Parental Rights and Duties and Custody Suits.*

025   **RAWSTRON D & CULLEN D (1986) *Child care law: a summary of the law in England and Wales* 2nd edition. BAAF. 36pp.
Summary of law on private and local authority care, children in care, adoption, wardship, and the courts.

026   SOUTHON V (1986) *Children in care: paying their new families*
DHSS. 317pp.
Review of attitudes and practices relating to the payment of foster parents and
adopters in Ontario, Manitoba, New York State, Denmark and West Germany.
Impressionistic account, but lively, refreshingly direct style: "In New York State the
quality of child care work is poor (because of the low calibre and morale of staff).
Social workers need the decision-making process to be easy, and don't question
whether the decision made is the right one. Permanency planning is simple but
inflexible, with no room for shades of grey; and it's illustrative of New York State's
focus on quantitative rather than qualitative factors in child care work."

GENERAL PRACTICE AND RESEARCH

The research base for policy and practice over the next few years is likely to
be the series of studies sponsored by the DHSS and summarised in their
1985 publication, *Social work decisions in child care*. The cumulative effect
of these studies is frankly depressing – with their evidence of reactive social
work practice, inadequate planning, poor communication, and so on – and
the reader is tempted to conclude either that there is no good practice
anywhere, or that researchers are not yet geared to identifying good practice
when they meet it. An important feature of these studies has been their
focus on agency policy and practice as much as on clients' situations. Any
study which seeks to explain why children come into care only by looking at
the children or their parents can now be seen as ignoring at least half the
story.
      Managers and practitioners concerned to sharpen up their decision
making will find much practical guidance in STEIN & RZEPNICKI (1983,
1984).

027   ALDGATE J (1980) 'Identification of factors influencing children's
length of stay in care' in J TRISELIOTIS (ed) *New developments in foster
care and adoption* Routledge & Kegan Paul, 22-40.
Research study identifying three important factors: the circumstances leading to
care; the maintenance of frequent contact between parents and children; and
purposeful social work activity.

028   BACON R & ROWE J (1978) *Substitute family care – a regional
study: 1 The use and misuse of resources* ABAFA. 15pp.
Report of a Children-Who-Wait-type study in one English region, looking
particularly at the planning and organisation of family placement services.
(See also 052.)

029   BAILY TF & BAILY WH (1983) *Child welfare practice: a guide to providing effective services for children and families* California: Jossey-Bass Inc. 243pp.
US introduction to the child welfare field, with chapters on intake and assessment, separation, day care, foster care and residential care, child protection, termination, advocacy and prevention. Brief annotated bibliography for each topic.

030   COOPER J (1978) *Patterns of family placement: current issues in fostering and adoption* National Children's Bureau. 119pp.
Descriptive account of some developments in foster care and adoption in the mid-1970s.

031   DENTON G (1984) *For whose eyes only? files and young people in care* National Association of Young People in Care. 15pp.
Report of a postal survey undertaken by NAYPIC of young people in care on issues around access to personal files.

032   **DEPARTMENT OF HEALTH AND SOCIAL SECURITY (1985) *Social work decisions in child care: recent research findings and their implications* DHSS 73pp.
An excellent publication providing abstracts of recent DHSS-sponsored research projects, an overview by Jane Rowe of major issues, and practical exercises for the implementation of the lessons in agency practice. See 014, 033, 045, 047, 053, 060, 178 and 229 for fuller references to the researches themselves.

033   *FISHER M, MARSH P, PHILLIPS D & SAINSBURY E (1986) *In and out of care: the experiences of children, parents and social workers* Batsford/BAAF. 154pp.
DHSS-sponsored study of 55 children in care in Sheffield, including interviews with social workers, parents and children, followed up over 12 months. The study highlights differences in the various parties' perceptions at each stage of the care process.

034   FITZGERALD J & MURCER B & B (1982) *Building new families through adoption and fostering* Basil Blackwell. 136pp.
Account of the philosophy and practice of a Children's Society Long-Stay Unit (St Luke's), where children are prepared for family placement.

035   GRUBER A (1978) *Children in foster care* NY: Human Sciences Press. 226pp.
Research study of almost 6,000 children in care of Massachusetts Department of Public Welfare in 1971. Almost one-quarter in care because of parental mental illness. 40% of children in foster homes disabled in some way. Little preventive/rehabilitative work, foster homes becoming permanent (foster care a poor people's programme), inadequate diagnostic/treatment services for children. Lengthy recommendations for improved service.

036   *HARTMAN A & VINOKUR-KAPLAN D (1987) 'Women and men working in child welfare: different voices' *Child Welfare* 64, 3, May/June, 307-314.
Study of social workers in child welfare confirms previous research indicating that men and women have different world-views. Significantly, men value separation whereas women value attachment. In this study, women ascribed greater importance to preservation of the family, prevention of admission to care, working towards reunification, and preventive outreach work. Men gave greater emphasis to working with involuntary clients and troubled adolescents, and to decision-making in child placement.

037   JAFFEE ED (1979) 'Computers in child placement planning' *Social Work* 24, 5, Sept, 380-385.
Study comparing case conference and computer recommendations for child placement. Discussion of the potential for computer assistance in placement decisions, with a note of caution against the risk of dehumanising the individual child.

038   JONES MA, NEUMAN R & SHERMAN A (1976) *A second chance for families – evaluation of a program to reduce foster care* NY: Child Welfare League of America. 133pp.
039   JONES MA (1985) *A second chance for families – five years later – follow-up of a program to prevent foster care* NY: Child Welfare League of America. 161pp.
Two-part US study involving families being randomly assigned to groups for 'ordinary' or 'special' social work help. The 1976 study showed that after 12 months a smaller proportion of children receiving specialist service came into care; they had higher 'wellbeing' ratings; and the parents' functioning was at a more satisfactory level. The 1985 follow-up study showed a tendency for many children to come into care after the withdrawal of special services, but they stayed in care for shorter periods than did those in the 'ordinary' group.

040   LAWSON A (1980) 'Taking the decision to remove the child from the family' *Journal of Social Welfare Law*, May, 141-163.
Study undertaken in Hertfordshire of children on the abuse register, comparing ten admitted to care with ten others not admitted.

041   MANN P (1984) *Children in care revisited* Batsford/BAAF. 199pp.
Account of interviews with 13 young people who were formerly on the author's caseload, discussing their subsequent reactions to and reflections on their care experiences.

042   **MARSH P, FISHER M & PHILLIPS D (1985) 'Negotiating child care: the experiences of workers and clients' *Adoption & Fostering* 9, 3, 11-17.
Article summarising the research described in FISHER et al (033).

043   McDONNELL P & ALDGATE J (1984) 'Review procedures for children in care' *Adoption & Fostering* 8, 3, 47-51.

044   McDONNELL P & ALDGATE J (1984) 'An alternative approach to reviews' *Adoption & Fostering* 8, 4, 47-51.
Two papers derived from the authors' research study of reviews on children in care. The first paper considers some of the findings and the professional and administrative aspects of reviews. The second paper takes the discussion further and offers an alternative approach to reviews, involving a two-tier system.

045   *MILLHAM S, BULLOCK R, HOSIE K & HAAK M (1986) *Lost in care: the problems of maintaining links between children in care and their families* Gower. 258pp.
DHSS-sponsored study of the links between parents and their children in care, exploring the nature of these links and problems in maintaining them. Extensive study of 450 children coming into the care of five local authorities supplemented by an intensive study of four children and their families.

046   NATIONAL ASSOCIATION OF YOUNG PEOPLE IN CARE (1984) *Leaving care – where?* NAYPIC. 47pp.
Conference papers including contributions on research (a summary of STEIN & CAREY's study – see 054), resources, housing and homelessness, and the Bradford After-Care Service, as well as a list of relevant resources.

047   *PACKMAN J, RANDALL J & JACQUES N (1986) *Who needs care? social-work decisions about children* Basil Blackwell. 221pp.
DHSS-sponsored study of children considered for admission to care in two English local authorities. No clear differences emerged initially between those admitted and those not admitted, though further analysis in terms of 'volunteers', 'victims' and 'villains' revealed interesting differences in the agencies' policies and practices. Use of admission to care only as a last resort found to be unhelpful, resulting in ill-planned, emergency admissions, and experienced as unhelpful by the families concerned.

048   PINE BA (1987) 'Strategies for more ethical decision making in child welfare practice' *Child Welfare* 66, 4, July/August, 315-326.
Using a case-illustration, the author sets out to demonstrate the usefulness of a model for helping to resolve ethical dilemmas in child welfare.

049   ROSENBLATT A & MAYER JE (1970) 'Reduction of uncertainty in child placement decisions' *Social Work* 15, 4, Oct, 52-59.
Authors examine some of the factors which serve to reduce the levels of stress experienced by child welfare workers – case responsibility restricted and shared, indulgence in excessive fact-gathering, the limited range of options available, and the difficulty of assessing the effectiveness of the worker's activity.

050   ST CLAIRE L & OSBORN AF (1987) 'The ability and behaviour of children who have been "in-care" or separated from their parents' *Early Child Development & Care* 28, 3, 187-354.
Comparative study of three groups: one of children who had been in care before the age of five years; a second group, never in care but separated from mother for at least a month before the age of five; and a control group. The average level of achievement of the in-care group was significantly lower than that of the controls even after adjustment for social background. Children who had been in residential care were at particularly high risk of anti-social behaviour disorder.

051   SCHAFFER HR (1985) 'Making decisions about children' *Adoption & Fostering* 9, 1, 22-28.
Review of the present state of research knowledge on child development relevant to children in care.

052   SHAW M & LEBENS K (1978) *Substitute family care – a regional study: II What shall we do with the children?* ABAFA. 27pp.
Research study focusing on social workers' attitudes to and assumptions about the options available for child placement. (See also 028.)

053   SINCLAIR R (1984) *Decision making in statutory reviews on children in care* Gower. 171pp.
DHSS-sponsored study of statutory review procedures in one local authority with recommendations for improvements in policy and practice. (See also 032.)

054   *STEIN M & CAREY K (1986) *Leaving care* Basil Blackwell. 189pp.
ESRC-sponsored study of young people (aged 16-18) leaving care in Wakefield and followed up over two-and-a-half years. Semi-structured interviews with the young people on their lives in care and subsequent experiences form the basis of concrete proposals for a 'leaving care' policy. An important conclusion is that it is often more realistic to prepare young people for *interdependent* than for *independent* living – given the experience of many young people in care, the 'bridge to independence' is perhaps a bridge too far.

055   STEIN M & ELLIS S (1983) *Gizza say? reviews and young people in care* National Association of Young People in Care. 9pp.
Survey by NAYPIC of young people's experiences of and responses to reviews.

056   STEIN M & MAYNARD C (1985) *I've never been so lonely* National Association of Young People in Care.
Consumer study by NAYPIC of the experiences of young people leaving care.

057 *STEIN TJ & RZEPNICKI TL (1983) *Decision making at child welfare intake: a handbook for practitioners* NY: Child Welfare League of America. 130pp.
"When treatment and nurturance . . . are the primary focus, foster care, rather than being a means to the end of reuniting children with their parents, can become an end in itself". As an alternative, the authors advocate a decision-making approach, and offer a systematic guide (with flow charts) to decision making at each stage in the intake process. Although addressed to US agencies, it translates readily to the UK scene.

058 *STEIN TJ & RZEPNICKI TL (1984) *Decision making in child welfare services: intake and planning* Mass: Kluwer-Nijhoff Publishing. 171pp.
Sequel to the authors' 1983 publication, this is concerned with intake decisions, on the premise that successful permanency planning is determined by the quality of the agency's initial responses to reports of a child at risk.

059 THOBURN J (1980) *Captive clients: social work with families of children home on trial* Routledge & Kegan Paul. 202pp.
Study in one English local authority of children living at home under care orders or supervision orders. Most important factor in the decision to let children return home or remain at home was the determination of most of the parents and of their children to stay together as family. Attitudes and skills of the social workers in mobilising necessary resources and the nature of the practical and emotional support offered were also important.

060 *VERNON J & FRUIN D (1986) *In care: a study of social work decision-making* National Children's Bureau. 157pp.
DHSS-sponsored study of decision making in relation to 185 children in 11 English local authorities. Researchers found worrying levels of non-decision-making in such key areas as parent-child contact in care, discharge from care, reviews and planning for children in care.

061 **WENDELKEN C (1983) *Children in and out of care* Heinemann. 119pp.
Offers principles of good child care practice at each stage of the care process, with useful checklists.

062 WHITTAKER JK (1986) 'Formal and informal helping in child welfare services: implications for management and practice' *Child Welfare* 65, 1, Jan/Feb, 17-25.
Argues for a less individualised, pathological view and a more ecological, systemic view of human development; and for the development and use of informal social networks in child welfare.

PERMANENCY AND DRIFT

The idea of permanency grew out of concern which began to be expressed during the 1960s regarding foster care 'drift', children growing up in long-term care with neither stability, continuity nor coherent planning for their future. The essence of permanency thinking is that 'care' is no place for a child to grow up, and that every effort should be geared towards getting children out of care, preferably to their families of origin, or, failing that, into adoptive families.

In the US, less so in the UK, the early advocates of permanency appeared to adopt GOLDSTEIN et al 1973 as their bible, though critics were quick to criticise this text for its extreme and over-simple approach to human relationships. Practitioners and policy makers in the UK were more immediately impressed by the publication, also in 1973, of ROWE & LAMBERT's *Children who wait*, which generated a degree of public and professional interest not seen since Dr John Bowlby's *Child care and the growth of love* in the 1950s.

Research interest in permanency has fallen broadly into three types: experimental projects intended to achieve permanency (eg STEIN *et al*; THOBURN *et al*); studies seeking to identify factors affecting the length of stay in care or the children's chances of being successfully restored to their families (eg BLOCK & LIBOWITZ, OLSEN, RZEPNICKI); and, more recently, studies of the outcome of permanency programmes (eg BARTH & BERRY, LAHTI, SELTZER & BLOKSBERG).

Critics of permanency thinking will have their worst fears confirmed by the growing evidence from outcome studies that adoption is proving to be the most likely (and most successful) course of action in permanency programmes. Whether MALUCCIO *et al*'s strong emphasis on work to restore children to their original families will operate as a new dispensation for parents in the 1990s remains to be seen. At any rate, MALUCCIO *et al* is by far the best introduction to the theory and practice of permanency planning.

063   ADCOCK M & WHITE R (eds) (1980) *Terminating parental contact: an exploration of the issues relating to children in care* ABAFA. 56pp.
Seminar papers by Richard White (legal aspects), Margaret Adcock (social work dilemmas), Christine Cooper (paediatric aspects) and Arnon Bentovim (psychiatric aspects).

064   BARTH RP & BERRY M (1987) 'Outcomes of child welfare services under permanency planning' *Social Service Review* 61,1, March, 71-90.
Review of permanency research indicates that adopted children do well, and even the less-favoured option of long-term fostering has its merits. However, children who are returned home do least well – and receive the poorest service.

065   BLOCK NM & LIBOWITZ AS (1983) *Recidivism in foster care* NY: Child Welfare League of America. 93pp.
Study of 338 children discharged from the care of the Jewish Child Care Association of New York. (For US writers on child welfare,'recidivism' means re-entry into care.) Children aged 13-15 were the most likely to return; those with siblings in care of the same agency less likely; higher rate of re-entry amongst those originally received for child-related reasons than those received for family-related reasons. Children in care for 'child' reasons and discharged to two-parent families the most likely group to return to care. Frequency and quality of parental visiting while in care important factors. Children discharged to adoptive homes did not return to care at all.

066   BRYER M (1988) *Planning in child care: a guide for team leaders and their teams* BAAF.
Addressed primarily to senior social workers and team leaders, this work-book is concerned with the management of planning rather than the skills and methods of working with children. Against a framework for planning which is set out at the beginning the author examines the various stages in working with children and families, from prevention to the point of discharge from care. Particular attention is paid to planning in relation to teenagers, now a substantial proportion of the care population.

067   BUSH M & GOLDMAN H (1982) 'The psychological parenting and permanency principles in child welfare: a reappraisal and critique' *American Journal of Orthopsychiatry* 52, 2, April, 223-235.
Critique of Goldstein *et al* 1973 on grounds of being simplistic, ignoring the views of children, and letting agencies too easily off the hook in the pursuit of prevention and rehabilitation.

068   CLARK B (1977) 'A cause for concern – child care policy and practice' *Social Work Today* 8,43, 9 August, 7-10.
Critical of the apparent switch in agency priorities from long-term fostering to adoption, a move which the author argues is not supported by research but is rather a response to bureaucratic needs, the adoption market, pressures to save money, and to the needs of social workers themselves.

069 FANSHEL D (1982) *On the road to permanency: an expanded data base for service to children in foster care* NY: Child Welfare League of America. 337pp.
Detailed computer analysis of the careers of children in care in New York City, with enough tables to satisfy any computaholic. The apparent willingness of NY social workers to rate parents on a continuum from 'responsible' to completely 'irresponsible' will not pass unnoticed by anyone who has read the disturbing report by SOUTHON (026).

070 FINCH SJ, FANSHEL D & GRUNDY JF (1986) 'Factors associated with the discharge of children from foster care' *Social Work Research & Abstracts* 22,1, 10-18.
Technical article on the use of a computerised data base to track children in care in New York City, seeking to identify factors associated with discharge from care.

071 **FOX LM (1982) 'Two value positions in recent child care law and practice' *British Journal of Social Work* 12, 3, 265-290.
Interesting theoretical analysis of the permanency debate in terms of 'kinship defenders' and 'society as parent' value positions.

072 FRIEDMAN RM, BARON A, LARDIERI S & QUICK J (1982) 'Length of time in foster care: a measure in need of analysis' *Social Work* 27, 6, Nov, 499-503.
Authors argue that caution needs to be exercised in using length of time in care as a measure of the success of a foster care programme.

073 GOLDSTEIN J, FREUD A & SOLNIT AJ (1973) *Beyond the best interests of the child* NY: Free Press. 171pp.
Classic, extreme statement of the case for recognising the primacy of the 'psychological' parent and the need for the speedy transfer to that parent of all legal rights and responsibilities so as to ensure the child's psychological wellbeing. Essential reading for students of permanency but not for parents of a nervous disposition. For rebuttal see 067, 077 and 080.

074 GOLDSTEIN J, FREUD A & SOLNIT AJ (1980) *Before the best interests of the child* Burnett Books/André Deutsch. 286pp.
Sequel to *Beyond . . .*, arguing for minimum State intervention and for the child's wellbeing to be the paramount consideration once intervention is under way.

075 *HOWE GW (1983) 'The ecological approach to permanency planning: an interactionist perspective' *Child Welfare* 62, 4, July/August, 291-301.
On the applicability of an interactionist approach in child care, and the dangers of 'attribution error' amongst professionals.

076   HUSSELL C & MONAGHAN B (1982) 'Going for good' *Social Work Today* 13, 47, 17 August, 7-9.
Account of the development and implementation of a permanency policy in Lambeth.

077   KADUSHIN A (1974) *'Beyond the best interests of the child*: an essay review' *Social Service Review* 48, 4, December, 508-516.
Critical of GOLDSTEIN *et al* 1973 for ignoring the genuine dilemmas social workers face in work with children and families, and in particular for oversimplifying the question of children's rights.

078   KRYMOW VL (1979) 'Obstacles encountered in permanent planning for foster children' *Child Welfare* 58, 2, Feb, 97-104.
The conflicting aims of security and continuity for children make for difficulty in reaching permanency decisions.

079   LAHTI J (1982) 'A follow-up study of foster children in permanent placements' *Social Service Review* 56, 4, Dec, 556-571.
Follow-up study of the Oregon Project intended to achieve permanency: adoption was the most stable in outcome, long-term fostering less so, rehabilitation with parents least of all. In terms of wellbeing, a sense of permanence was the single most important factor – perception of permanence being more important than actual legal status.

080   MAHONEY K & MAHONEY MJ (1974) 'Psychoanalytic guidelines for child placement' *Social Work* 19, 6, Nov, 688-696.
Critique of GOLDSTEIN *et al* 1973, whose theory is found wanting in the face of the empirical evidence.

081   **MALUCCIO AN, FEIN E & OLMSTEAD KA (1986) *Permanency planning for children: concepts and methods* Tavistock. 328pp.
Likely to be the standard text on permanency for a considerable time, with its theoretical analysis and detailed practice guidelines for work with parents and children.

082   OLSEN LJ (1982) 'Predicting the permanency status of children in foster care' *Social Work Research & Abstracts* 18, 9-20.
Ohio study of placement careers of children over an 18-month period. Children over eight years of age tended to be seen as unadoptable; ethnic minority children were less likely to be adopted; and children with handicaps also waited longer for permanent placement.

083 *PARKER RA (1985) 'Planning into practice' *Adoption & Fostering* 9, 4, 25-28.
Paper on planning for children in care, stressing the need to attend to the nature of the support for and opposition to a particular plan; to acknowledge that plans will sometimes fail; and to undertake contingency planning.

084 ROONEY RH (1982) 'Permanency planning: boon for all children?' *Social Work* 27, 2, March, 152-8.
Critique of the use of permanency as a panacea for children in long-term care.

085 **ROWE J & LAMBERT L (1973) *Children who wait* ABAA. 195pp.
Now classic study of children in care indicating that a considerable number of children remain in long-term care with little chance of returning home; and that many of these children are inappropriately placed, there being little evidence of positive planning for their care.

086 *RZEPNICKI TL (1987) 'Recidivism of foster children returned to their own homes: a review and new directions for research' *Social Service Review* 61, 1, March, 56-70.
With greater emphasis now on reuniting children with their families, there is concern that rates of re-entry into care may be on the increase. After reviewing the data currently available, the author seeks to identify specific areas where more information is needed for the design of more effective services to achieve stability after reunification. The author finds evidence of substantial difficulties for many children and families after the return home and deficiencies in the services which families are offered.

087 SEABERG JR & TOLLEY ES (1986) 'Predictors of the length of stay in foster care' *Social Work Research & Abstracts* 22, 3, 11-17.
Technical article on the use of statistical models to identify relevant factors, different factors becoming significant depending on the model in use.

088 *SELTZER MM & BLOKSBERG LM (1987) 'Permanency planning and its effects on foster children: a review of the literature' *Social Work* 32, 1, Jan/Feb, 65-68.
Review of relevant US research indicates higher rate of adoption achieved in agencies where permanency planning philosophy accepted than where it is not; adoptions tend to be stable, while a substantial minority of rehabilitations are not – rate of disruption from rehabilitation seems to be no lower since permanency planning than before; no evident differences in children's adjustment between those in permanent and those in temporary placements.

089   SHERMAN EA, NEUMAN R & SHYNE AW (1973) *Children adrift in foster care: a study of alternative approaches* NY: Child Welfare League of America. 129pp.
Study of 413 children assigned (non-randomly) to 'ordinary' or to 'special service' groups. No evidence of better discharge rates in the 'special' group, rather the reverse, though there was a lower frequency of re-entry to care for this group. Link between level of parental visiting and early discharge.

090   SOSIN MR (1987) 'Delivery services under permanency planning' *Social Service Review* 61, 2, June, 272-290.
Wisconsin study suggesting that permanency is more readily achieved in agencies in which workers make use of many sources of information in planning, less readily achieved where workers frequently focus on adoption in their contacts with natural parents. Quite a technical paper with a simple moral: it is best to focus on the tangible and realistic.

091   STEIN TJ, GAMBRILL ED & WILTSE KT (1978) *Children in foster homes: achieving continuity of care* NY: Praeger. 280pp.
Account of research undertaken in the Alameda Project, involving intensive work to achieve permanency and an evaluation of the effectiveness of a systematic case management procedure, using behavioural methods. Excellent chapter on decision making.

092   THOBURN J, MURDOCH A & O'BRIEN A (1986) *Permanence in child care* Blackwell. 202pp.
Research study into the Children's Society project, *The Child Wants a Home*.

093   TURNER J (1983) 'High risk decision making' *Adoption & Fostering* 7, 4, 19-23.
Case study demonstrating intensive work to achieve permanence through restoration of the child to the family.

094   TURNER J (1984) 'Predictors of recidivism in foster care: exploratory models' *Social Work Research & Abstracts* 20, 2, Summer, 15-20.
Technical article discussing the use of eight different models intended to predict the likelihood or otherwise of children returning to foster care after discharge. Only one model seemed moderately useful.

095   TURNER J (1986) 'Successful reunification of foster care children with their biological parents: characteristics of parents and children' *Child Care Quarterly* 15, 1,Spring, 50-54.
Comparative study of 50 children successfully reunited with their parents after foster care and 50 children who returned to foster care following their return home. Families with multiple problems and those requesting their child's initial placement in care are more at risk of 'recidivism' than others. Also physical and/or mental health problems in the parents significant. The fact that many children were 'rehabilitated' prior to improvement in family problems has implications for case management.

096   *VERNON J (1985) 'Planning for children in care?' *Adoption & Fostering* 9, 1, 13-17.
Summary of research findings in VERNON & FRUIN 1986 (see 060).

097   WOLSTENHOLME E (1984) 'Using information on children in care' *Adoption & Fostering* 8, 4, 21-23.
Account of the development and implementation of a policy on gatekeeping and permanence in Bradford, involving a partnership between social work practice and management information.

PLACEMENT BREAKDOWN AND DISRUPTION

Until relatively recently, placement breakdown – like death, and for similar reasons – was rarely discussed, and then only in hushed tones. The recent attention given to this topic is an acknowledgement of the fact that, if family placement services are seriously to take on board the 'hard-to-place' child, there will inevitably be more risk of placements going wrong.

Whoever first applied the term 'disruption' to family placement, it was Kay Donley who brought it to the notice of social workers in the UK (DONLEY 1977, 1978). The change in terminology was intended to remove the overtones of doom and failure implicit in the term 'breakdown', and to encourage the belief that the premature ending of a placement should not be thought of as signalling the end of the world, or even the end of planning for a child's family placement. Whether a placement disruption feels any less awful to those directly involved than a breakdown used to is perhaps an open question. Nevertheless, a greater willingness to regard premature endings not as an embarrassing mess but rather as an experience which everyone involved may learn from seems to hold out more hope for the future. Of the references offered below, FITZGERALD is the obvious starting-point, while ALDGATE & HAWLEY and BERRIDGE & CLEAVER provide much interesting material and discussion.

098   ABAFA (1977) *Looking back on disruption: breakdown in family placements* ABAFA. 16pp.
Papers from a workshop presented by Spaulding for Children, Michigan.

099   *ALDGATE J & HAWLEY D (1986) *Recollections of disruption: a study of foster care breakdowns* NFCA. 76pp.
Oxfordshire study of 11 long-term placements which had terminated prematurely between 1976 and 1980. Information was obtained from files, social workers and foster parents on the disruption, the effect of disruption on the foster family, preparation for placement, and the placement itself.

100   *ALDGATE J & HAWLEY D (1986) 'Helping foster families through disruption' *Adoption & Fostering* 10, 2, 44-49 & 58.

101   *ALDGATE J & HAWLEY D (1986) 'Preventing disruption in long-term foster care' *Adoption & Fostering* 10, 3, 23-30.
Two papers based on material gathered for the study noted above.

102   ALDRIDGE MJ & CAUTLEY PW (1975) The importance of worker availability in the functioning of new foster homes' *Child Welfare* 54, 6, June, 444-453.
Study suggesting that adequate preparation for placement is a good investment of workers' time and energy and that inadequate preparation cannot readily be compensated for later. Especially in new foster homes, the worker's early involvement is more efficient and more likely to produce positive results than efforts at a later stage when the worker perceives that things are not going well. The willingness of the worker to be available (by visits, or just by returning telephone calls) is significantly related not only to the attitude of both foster parents, but to their satisfaction with their new role and their morale generally.

103   BARTH RP, BERRY M, CARLSON ML, GOODFIELD R & FEINBERG B (1986) 'Contributors to disruption and dissolution of older-child adoptions' *Child Welfare* 65, 4, July/Aug, 359-371.
In the light of indications that the placement of 'hard-to-place' children is leading to some increase in adoption disruptions, the authors review recent research in an attempt to identify the main factors leading to disruption.

104   BELLWOOD P (1982) 'Disruption reviews in fostering' *Adoption & Fostering* 6, 1, 37-42.
Discusses the disruption review as a forum for discovering why some placements break down, and for increasing inter-agency understanding of the problems of fostering.

105   BERRIDGE D & CLEAVER H (1986) *A study of fostering break-downs* University of Bristol Dartington Social Research Unit. 21pp.
ESRC-sponsored study to determine the incidence, causes and predictability of breakdown. The research combined an extensive study of 530 placements and an intensive study of ten placements in two social services departments and one voluntary agency. Interviews with social workers, foster parents, natural parents, children and (surely a welcome innovation?) school teachers. Discussion of preliminary findings, to be developed in BERRIDGE & CLEAVER 1987 (106).

106   BERRIDGE D & CLEAVER H (1987) *Foster home breakdown* Basil Blackwell. 234pp.
See note on 105.

107   DEVON CC SOCIAL SERVICES DEPARTMENT RESEARCH AND TRAINING SECTION (1982) 'Fostering in South Devon – a study of terminations of placement in 1980-81' *Clearing House for Local Authority Social Services Research* no 6, 28 August, 11-58.
Study of all foster home placements in South Devon terminating between April 1980 and March 1981 showed a relatively high failure rate among short-term placements, with around one-third ending in breakdown. Child behaviour or personality problems were the factors most commonly recorded. Other factors included children with handicaps, foster parent control/discipline issues, and relations with birth parents. Half the placements intended to be long-term ended in breakdown, often within the first year or first few months.

108   DONLEY K (1978) 'The dynamics of disruption' *Adoption & Fostering* 2, 2, 34-39.
Discussion of the causes, treatment and effects of disruption.

109   FESTINGER T (1986) *Necessary risk: a study of adoptions and disrupted adoptive placements* NY: Child Welfare League of America. 48pp.
US study of 897 children over the age of six when 12 months into placement. Long-term disruption rate estimated to be about 13%. Risk factors included sharing the home with adoptive parents' own children of the opposite sex, and being placed alone rather than with siblings. Older children were also more at risk of disruption.

110   *FITZGERALD J (1983) *Understanding disruption* BAAF. 48pp.
Handbook on the management of disruption, based on the experience of the Adoption Resource Exchange.

111   PARDECK JT (1982) *The forgotten children: a study of the stability and continuity of foster care* Washington DC: University Press of America. 102pp.
US study of over 4000 children in the care of public agencies which found higher levels of placement stability than might be expected – over 75% of children were in their first or second placement. Placement stability was greater for black than for white children. Placements of offenders were no more unstable than those of non-offenders.

112   ROBINSON M (1985) 'Brief intervention to prevent fostering breakdown' *Adoption & Fostering* 9, 3, 17-23.
Case presentation by an independent social worker.

113   ROWE J (1987) 'Fostering outcomes: interpreting breakdown rates' *Adoption & Fostering* 11, 1, 32-34 & 25.
Article on the problems of defining and measuring breakdown, with a reminder of a basic question in research, "Am I comparing like with like?".

114   ZWIMPFER DM (1983) 'Indicators of adoption breakdown' *Social Casework* 64, 3, March, 169-177.
New Zealand study of adoptive placements comparing some which broke down with others that did not. In the 'breakdown' group, contra-indications had emerged during the adoptive home study, and the practice of 'matching for marginality' (marginal applicants for marginal children) was seen to be operating.

SOCIAL WORK WITH CHILDREN – GENERAL

Attempting to interview children provides social workers and other professionals with some of their most embarrassing moments. For this reason, one of the most exciting and useful developments in the last ten years or so has been the flow of material on communicating and working with children. From the full-scale training packs of BAAF to the slim pamphlet by the CATHOLIC CHILDREN'S SOCIETY, social workers can now draw upon a wide range of material, including games, exercises and ideas for playwork with children. The widespread interest in the life-story book as a means of helping children make sense of their history is reflected in several publications listed here, only a sample of the many currently available. The starting-point in this list, invaluable for anyone concerned with children in crisis, is JEWETT.

115   ABAFA (1977) *Planning for children in long-term care* Teacher's notes and student pack. ABAFA.
Training material on children who wait, identifying and planning for children, working with natural parents, children and substitute families, and planning placements.

116   ABAFA (1977) *Working with children who are joining new families* Training aid and teacher's handbook. ABAFA.
Training material with sections on seeing the child as client, preparing a plan, helping the child to understand his or her past, exploring ways of communicating with children, preparing for placement, managing the move, child development, and life story books. Papers by Kay Donley, Pamela Mann and others.

117   ALDGATE J & SIMMONDS J (eds) (1987) *Direct work with children: a guide for social work practitioners* Batsford/BAAF. 148pp
Collection of papers on various aspects of direct work, the theoretical discussion illustrated by examples from practice by students on the Advanced Diploma in Social Work with Children and Families at Goldsmith's College.

118   ALTON H & FIRMIN C (1987) *Moving pictures* BAAF.
Pack containing sets of pictures for social workers, foster parents and adoptive parents to use in helping children come to terms with placement moves or other significant features of their lives.

119   AUST PH (1981) 'Using the life story book in treatment of children in placement' *Child Welfare* 60, 8 ,Sept/Oct, 535-560.
Description of the use of the life story book to enhance child's self-image.

120 BAAF (1984) *In touch with children* BAAF.
Substantial pack of training materials on all aspects of working with children.

121   **BAAF (1986) *Working with children – practice papers* BAAF. 120pp.
Collection of papers used in training pack *In touch with children* on child development and direct work with children.

122   BUSH M & GORDON AC (1982) 'The case for involving children in child welfare decisions' *Social Work* 27, 4, July, 309-314.
Argues the case for involving children in planning and decision making, on grounds of efficacy as well as ethics. Stresses the need to take account of the power imbalance between children and adult professionals.

123   *CATHOLIC CHILDREN'S SOCIETY (1983) *Finding out about me: games for the preparation of children for family placement* Surrey: Catholic Children's Society. 22p.
Derived from practice experience in the Society's Homefinding Unit at Gravesend.

124   CENTRAL COUNCIL FOR EDUCATION AND TRAINING IN SOCIAL WORK (1978) *Good enough parenting: report of a group on work with children and young people and the implications for social work education* CCETSW. 192pp.
Wide-ranging collection of papers, largely focusing on direct work with children.

125   CONNOR T, SCLARE I, DUNBAR D & ELLIFFE J (1985) 'Making a life story book' *Adoption & Fostering* 9, 2, 32-35 & 46.
Account of the use of life story books at 'Familymakers' Homefinding Unit at Gravesend.

126   **CROMPTON M (1980) *Respecting children: social work with young people* Edward Arnold. 246pp.
Ways of communicating with children through music, books and art as well as verbally.

127   DONLEY K (1979) 'Cover story' *Adoption & Fostering* 3, 1, 51-52.
Brief note on an indispensable but often neglected item of the fostered or adopted child's equipment for dealing with the outside world.

128   *FAHLBERG V (1981) *Attachment and separation* BAAF. 60pp.
Workbook dealing with attachment (and its assessment), separation, and the identification and resolution of attachment problems.

129   *FAHLBERG V (1981) *Helping children when they must move* BAAF. 101pp.
Workbook dealing with a variety of moves – in and out of care, between placements, into adoption – and the appropriate use of lifebooks and other tools.

130   **FAHLBERG V (1982) *Child development* BAAF. 99pp.
Workbook on 'normal' child development with attention also to issues of particular relevance to children in care.

131   FINKELSTEIN NE (1980) 'Children in limbo' *Social Work* 25, 2, March, 100-105.
Author looks at interventive strategies for six categories of children in care: those with committed families; those whose families are committed intellectually only; those without roots; those with roots but who cannot live at home; those with committed families judged unfit by society; and adolescents too old to return to own families or to seek permanence in a substitute family.

132   **JEWETT CL (1984) *Helping children cope with separation and loss* Batsford/BAAF. 146pp.
Clear, practical, down-to-earth guide for anyone concerned with children experiencing separation and loss.

133   KAGAN RM (1980) 'Using redefinition and paradox with children in placement who provoke rejection' *Child Welfare* 59, 9, Nov, 551-559.
Use of strategic family therapy technique of paradoxical injunction in child care cases.

134   LIGHTBOWN C (1979) 'Life story books' *Adoption & Fostering* 3, 3, 9-15.
Discussion of issues around the making of life story books.

135   LISHMAN J (ed)(1983) *Working with children* Research Highlights no.6, University of Aberdeen Department of Social Work. Scottish Academic Press.162pp.
Collection including papers on communicating with children, group work and direct work during foster family placement.

136   MARTEL S (ed) (1981) *Direct work with children* Bedford Square Press/NCVO. 95pp.
Collection of six papers mainly on play therapy and family group work.

137   NATIONAL ASSOCIATION OF YOUNG PEOPLE IN CARE (1979) *Running an in care group* NAYPIC.
An action pack of ideas, hints and suggestions for young people and social workers.

138   PAGE R & CLARK GA (eds) (1977) *Who cares? young people in care speak out* National Children's Bureau. 63pp.
Report of a series of NCB workshops for young people in care, which led to the setting up of Who Cares? groups in many local authority areas and eventually to the foundation of the National Association of Young People in Care (NAYPIC).

139   PARDECK JT & PARDECK JA (1987) 'Bibliotherapy for children in foster care and adoption' *Child Welfare* 66, 3, May/June, 269-278.
Discussion of the uses and limitations of bibliotherapy for helping children adjust to foster care and adoption experiences. Includes some suggested (US) books for children.

140   RYAN T & WALKER R (1985) *Making life story books* BAAF. 48pp.
Practice guide to making and using life story books, with examples.

SOCIAL WORK WITH PARENTS – GENERAL

Although the list of titles given in this section does not tell the whole story on 'working with parents' – see also the relevant sections in FOSTER FAMILY CARE and ADOPTION – there is no denying that parents have a small and somewhat limited share of the child welfare literature as compared with children themselves and other caregivers. It may be that the level of attention which parents receive in the literature simply reflects the position they occupy in practice. Nonetheless, it is salutary to contrast the creativity and imagination being brought to bear on 'communicating with children' (as evidenced by the previous section) with the relative neglect of this issue in relation to parents. An outsider may be tempted to conclude that communicating with parents is relatively easy, rather than, as any practitioner will agree, one of the most problematic aspects of child welfare practice.

There is also something relentless about the unblinking focus on parents solely in their roles as parents, as though they have no existence beyond that of providers (or, more often, non-providers) for their children. Again, this one-dimensional view may be an accurate reflection of how parents are perceived by agencies, and may go some way towards explaining the seemingly insoluble communication problems. As regards the literature on birth parents, there seems to be no equivalent to JEWETT on children (130), a sad and serious gap. MALUCCIO et al (081) or the collection edited by SINANOGLU & MALUCCIO (208) are perhaps the best starting-points.

141   ADCOCK M (1983) 'Working with natural parents to prevent long-term care' *Adoption & Fostering* 7, 3, 8-12.
Discussion of practice issues.

142   *ADCOCK M & WHITE R (eds) (1985) *Good-enough parenting: a framework for assessment* BAAF. 115pp.
Collection of papers drawn from BAAF *In touch with parents* (see 143). Topics include assessing parenting; standards of parenting and the law; parenting and parenting failure; good-enough and bad-enough parenting; predicting a family's response to treatment; also checklists on attachment, a chart illustrating the developmental progress of infants and young children, and a 'childhood level of living' scale and 'maternal characteristics' scale devised by Norman Polansky.

143   *BAAF (1984) *In touch with parents* BAAF.
Training materials for working with parents.

144   DIMMOCK B & DUNGWORTH D (1985) 'Beyond the family: using network meetings with statutory child care cases' *Journal of Family Therapy* 7, 45-68.
Using two case examples, the authors discuss the use of a 'network' approach.

145   GABINET L (1983) 'Shared parenting: a new paradigm for the treatment of child abuse' *Child Abuse & Neglect* 7, 403-411.
Advocates a range of 'shared parenting' facilities, including foster family care, in work with parents who have abused their children.

146   GIBBS J & THORPE R (1975) 'The natural parent group: an alternative to "parent bashing" ' *Social Work Today* 6, 13, 2 Oct, 386-389.
Account of a group for natural parents of children in care.

147   ISAAC BC, MINTY EB & MORRISON RM (1986) 'Children in care – the association with mental disorder in the parents' *British Journal of Social Work* 16, 325-339.
Study suggesting mental illness may be a factor in a significant proportion of parents whose children enter care.

148   MILLER J & COOK T (eds) (1981) *Direct work with families* Bedford Square Press. 144pp.
Nine papers with emphasis on severely disadvantaged and disorganised families.

149   *QUINTON D & RUTTER M (1984) 'Parents with children in care: I current circumstances and parenting; II intergenerational continuities' *Child Psychology & Psychiatry* 25, 2, 211-229; 231-250.
Detailed comparative study of two groups of families, one with a child admitted to care and the other 'intact', 95 families in all. "Parenting cannot be seen as an attribute of individuals irrespective of their current circumstances."

150   *WHITE R (1983) 'Written agreements with families' *Adoption & Fostering* 7, 4, 24-28.
Lawyer's view of the negotiation of 'contracts' with parents.

151   WOLF S (1987) 'Prediction in child care' *Adoption & Fostering* 11, 1, 11-17.
Paper on the psychiatric disorders in parents which have a damaging effect on their parenting capacity.

2 Foster family care

GENERAL

The most striking feature of foster family care is its ambiguous position within child welfare. Historically, its popularity with professionals and public alike has waxed and waned with sometimes remarkable speed and frequency since World War II (see PACKMAN 1981 - 009 - for the historical background). The early enthusiasm for placing children with foster parents as a means of 'rescuing' them from institutional care gave way to disenchantment in the face of high levels of placement breakdown. Later interest in 'preventive' work and in reuniting children with their families seemed to leave little room for fostering, with its attendant risks to links between child and birth family. The remarkable rise in the status of foster parents since the mid-1970s was accompanied by growing unease and eventual disenchantment with long-term fostering: with its inherent instability and uncertain division of responsibilities between birth parents, foster parents and agency, it came to be regarded by advocates of permanency as an unsatisfactory mode of care for children.

As well as having an ambiguous position within the overall child welfare system, foster family care is marked by substantial uncertainties as to aims, roles and tasks within the individual placement. With the recognition that foster care is an umbrella term for a wide range of activities, some useful work has been undertaken in the last ten years or so in identifying varieties of foster care and their related tasks. (The tendency amongst US writers to include residential care within 'foster care' only confuses matters further!) It is probably no coincidence that the notable developments in this field over the past decade have been in 'specialist' fostering, where a good deal of effort has gone into defining the aims, roles and tasks of all the parties involved. 'Specialist' fostering literature is dealt with later. The best starting-points in the general fostering literature are probably, for an introduction to current issues, the collection of papers edited by TRISELIOTIS; and, in relation to practice, the publication by DHSS, supplemented by HOREJSI. Special mention must be made of GEORGE, getting on for 20 years old, but still 'contemporary' in its treatment of issues which refuse to go away.

152 BAAF (1985) *Foster care: some questions answered* BAAF.
Leaflet giving brief general information about fostering.

153 COX MJ & COX RD (eds)(1985) *Foster care: current issues, policies and practices* New Jersey: Ablex Publishing Corp. 245pp.
Papers on US historical and legislative background; computerised information systems (Fanshel); permanency planning (Maluccio *et al*); cultural and racial issues; and foster parent training.

154 **DEPARTMENT OF HEALTH AND SOCIAL SECURITY (1976) *Foster care: a guide to practice* DHSS. 227pp.
Useful introduction to most aspects of foster care practice, although the material on foster parents in particular has been overtaken by later developments.

155 DINNAGE R & PRINGLE MLK (1967) *Foster home care: facts and fallacies* Longmans. 268pp.
Review of research in the US, Western Europe (including the UK) and Israel, 1948-1966.

156 *EASTMAN KS (1982) 'Sources of ambiguity in the foster care system' *Smith College Studies in Social Work* 52,3,June, 234-246.
Discussion of the ambiguities in foster care (some remediable, others not) which create difficulties in decision making.

157 EASTMAN KS (1985) 'Foster families: a comprehensive bibliography' *Child Welfare* 64,6,Nov/Dec, 565-585.
US bibliography covering a wide range of professional and 'popular' sources, unusual in including some UK material.

158 GEORGE V (1970) *Foster care: theory and practice* Routledge & Kegan Paul. 251pp.
Classic study indicating the gap between fostering theory and practice. Argues strongly the need to give much greater consideration to the place of birth parents and to reassess role of foster parents within the foster care system.

159 *HOGHUGHI M & HIPGRAVE T (1985) *Towards a discipline of fostering* NFCA. 32pp.
Two papers arguing for and seeking to provide a theoretical basis for fostering practice.

160 HOLMAN R (1973) *Trading in children: a study of private fostering* Routledge & Kegan Paul. 349pp.
Surprisingly, the only major study of privately fostered children, a substantial but often overlooked part of the child care population.

161   HOLMAN R (1975) 'The place of fostering in social work' *British Journal of Social Work* 5,1, 3-29.
Critique of the Children Act 1975 including the author's formulation of the ideas of 'inclusive' and 'exclusive' fostering. A shortened version of this paper – entitled 'Exclusive and inclusive concepts of fostering' – appears in 182.

162   **HOREJSI CR (1979) *Foster family care: a handbook for social workers, allied professionals, and concerned citizens* Springfield, Illinois: Charles C Thomas. 357pp.
Not everyone will like the question-and-answer style of presentation, but this is nonetheless a very handy guide to all aspects of foster family care.

163   IRISH FOSTER CARE ASSOCIATION (1984) *Open door – an introduction to foster care in the Republic of Ireland* Dublin: IFCA. 109pp.
Lively illustrated guide to foster family care.

164   KLINE D & OVERSTREET HMF (1972) *Foster care of children: nurture and treatment* NY: Columbia University Press. 316pp.
Useful text on the theory and practice of foster family care.

165   KUFELDT K (1979) 'Temporary foster care' *British Journal of Social Work* 9,1, 49-66.
Author argues the need to develop alternative models of practice so as to improve outcomes in temporary foster family care. Surveys relevant literature and seeks to develop a theoretical framework around issues of separation experience, the place of the natural family and role clarification.

166   LINDSEY D (1982) 'Achievements for children in foster care' *Social Work* 27,6, 491-496.
Takes a positive view of the potential for improvements in service for children from a review of three research studies, including the Alameda and Oregon permanence projects.

167   MEYER CH (1985) 'A feminist perspective on foster family care: a redefinition of the categories' *Child Welfare* 64, 3, May/June, 249-258.
Writer argues that only when foster family care is transformed from a 'pretend' natural family home into an efficient social service will it have an impact on the work done in child welfare.

168   MURRAY L (1984) 'A review of selected foster care-adoption research from 1978 to mid-1982' *Child Welfare* 63,2,March/April, 113-124.
Summary review of US research relating to permanency planning, adoption outcomes, foster parents, and 'recidivism' in foster care.

169   NAPIER H (1972) 'Success and failure in foster care' *British Journal of Social Work* 2,2, 187-204.
Study of fostering undertaken in one area of Lancashire during the period 1966-1971. Sample of 50 children whose placements lasted for at least five years (deemed 'successful') and 29 children whose placements broke down. Factors in success/failure related to previous work by TRASLER (see 233), PARKER (173) and GEORGE (158). Author notes that in almost every case, regardless of child's circumstances, there was at least a 50% chance of success.

170   NATIONAL FOSTER CARE ASSOCIATION (1976) *Faces of fostering* NFCA. 48pp.
Short accounts by children, natural parents and foster parents of their experiences of fostering.

171   NATIONAL FOSTER CARE ASSOCIATION (1986) *A review of the Children Act 10 years on – its effect on foster care policy and practice* NFCA. 44pp.
Conference papers by David Owen, Jane Tunstill, Tom White, John Triseliotis and Jane Rowe.

172   PARKER RA (1966) *Decision in child care: a study of prediction in fostering* Allen & Unwin. 121pp.
Classic research study which sought to develop a prediction table for success and failure in foster family placement.

173   PARKER RA (1978) 'Foster care in context' *Adoption & Fostering* 2,3, 27-32.
Discussion of issues and trends in foster care in the late 1970s.

174   PROSSER H (1978) *Perspectives on foster care* National Foundation for Educational Research. 244pp.
Review of fostering research 1967-1976.

175   ROONEY RH, MOORE LM & ROSENZWEIG K (1984) 'The foster care system simulation: evaluation of a training innovation' *Children & Youth Services Review* 6, 173-194.
Account of a foster care simulation exercise, with the tentative conclusion that it may have had an effect on the subsequent real-life behaviour of the participants.

176   ROWE J (1977) *Fostering in the 70s and beyond – a descriptive analysis of the current scene* ABAFA. 8pp. Reprinted in J TRISELIOTIS (ed) (1980) – see 182.
177   **ROWE J (1983) *Fostering in the eighties* BAAF. 40pp.
Discussion papers on issues current in foster care during the 1970s and early 1980s.

178 *ROWE J, CAIN H, HUNDLEBY M & KEANE A (1984) *Long-term foster care* Batsford/BAAF. 255pp.
Research study of 200 children fostered long-term in five local authorities, making use of case records and interviews with social workers, foster parents and children. Researchers conclude that, with all its defects, there is a future for long-term fostering, particularly for older children who have strong bonds with their natural families. Contrary to the conventional wisdom, placements with relatives were among the most successful of the placements studied. (See also 229.)

179 RUSSELL J (1986) 'The dynamics of authority in permanent substitute families' *Adoption & Fostering* 10,3, 31-35.
Argues that, particularly in relation to disruption, the nature of authority as expressed in the substitute family's way of life and basic rules has not received the attention it deserves.

180 SHAW M & LEBENS K (1976) 'Children between families: a study of foster home care at the introduction of the Children Bill 1975' *Adoption & Fostering* 84, 17-27.
Research study of children boarded out in one English local authority indicated that rehabilitation and parental contact have a low priority amongst social workers; also, a lack of communication between workers and foster parents on the question of adoption.

181 SOCIAL WORK SERVICE (1981) *A study of the boarding out of children* DHSS.
Report on the inspection of foster family care in 32 English local authorities and three voluntary child care organisations. While noting innovative and exciting developments in some authorities, the report gave no room for complacency: there were deficiencies in policy, management, supervision and practice, with frequent failures to meet even the minimum requirements of the Boarding Out Regulations.

182 **TRISELIOTIS J (ed)(1980) *New developments in foster care and adoption* Routledge & Kegan Paul. 243pp.
Excellent introduction to this field, with papers on children in care, issues in foster care, fostering teenagers, family placement of 'hard-to-place' children, &c.

NATURAL/BIRTH PARENTS IN FOSTER FAMILY CARE

"One of the fundamental issues that has to be resolved before any major headway is made in foster care is the part which natural parents should play in the lives of their children placed in foster homes" (GEORGE 1970: 218-9). The issue remains far from resolved. The literature in this area of child welfare addresses itself largely to three questions: is continuing parent-child contact necessary/important in facilitating the child's eventual return to the family of origin? (answer: yes); is parent-child contact important for the child's well-being, even if there is no prospect of a return home? (answers range from an emphatic 'yes' to 'no, unless such contact does not hinder permanency planning'); how is it possible to sustain parent-child contact when a child is in foster family care for any significant length of time? (answer: only with extreme difficulty, if at all).

The issues around visiting and contact generally between parents and their children in care are well covered in SINANOGLU & MALUCCIO, which includes the papers by COLON and LITTNER listed separately. A positive approach to involving parents – beyond mere 'contact' or 'visiting' – is to be found in BLUMENTHAL & WEINBERG. GIBSON & PARSLOE and MARSH offer interesting papers more directly applicable to the UK scene.

183   BARBER S (1985) 'Planning access to children in care' *Adoption & Fostering* 9,3, 26-32.
Using case examples, the author offers a step-by-step analysis of the process of planning and implementing access, and argues the importance of careful planning in view of the emotive nature of the issues involved.

184   *BLUMENTHAL K & WEINBERG A (eds)(1984) *Establishing parent involvement in foster care agencies* NY: Child Welfare League of America. 247pp.
After discussion on the importance of parental involvement, the authors examine the implications for staff at all levels in agencies in relation to individual work, case management, inter-agency co-operation, supervision and training. Useful appendices provide examples of agency documentation on placement agreements, case reviews and policies geared to parental involvement in a number of North American states. Useful annotated bibliography.

185   COLON F (1978) 'Family ties and child placement' *Family Process* 17,3,Sept, 289-312.
Argues the case for maintaining strong links between children and birth parents (or at least ensuring knowledge of origins) in situations of divorce, foster care and adoption.

186   *CRETNEY S (1984) 'Access orders in the juvenile court: the legal framework' *Adoption & Fostering* 8,3, 15-18
Discussion of access legislation and the code of practice from a legal standpoint.

187   DEPARTMENT OF HEALTH AND SOCIAL SECURITY (1983) *Code of practice on access to children in care* HMSO.

188 *FAMILY RIGHTS GROUP (1986) *Promoting links: keeping children and families in touch* Family Rights Group. 127pp.
Pamphlet on the importance and problems of maintaining good links between parents and their children in care. Includes a statement of the law on access, some relevant research, accounts of parents' difficulties in maintaining contact, and contributions from a social work practitioner, a foster parent and a councillor.

189 **GIBSON P & PARSLOE P (1984) 'What stops parental access to children in care' *Adoption & Fostering* 8,1, 18-24.
Results of a study initiated by the Family Rights Group into the reasons for the often poor levels of contact between parents and children in care, despite research evidence showing the value of good contact.

190 GIBSON TL, TRACY GS & DeBORD MS (1984) 'An analysis of variables affecting length of stay in foster care' *Children & Youth Services Review* 6, 135-145.
Study suggesting the importance not only of the actual amount of parent-child contact but also where the initiative for contact comes from: if initiated by the family, fewer contacts are necessary to enable the child to return home within a month than if the agency has to take the initiative. Intensive and frequent agency-family contact may be necessary at the beginning of the placement if the child is to return home.

191 HESS P & WILLIAMS LB (1982) 'Group orientation for parents of children in foster family care' *Child Welfare* 61,7,Sept/Oct, 456-466.
Account of a group organised by an agency in Tennessee to induct natural parents into their expected roles and support them in the process of deciding their children's future.

192 HESS PM & PROCH K (1986) 'How the states regulate parent-child visiting' *Public Welfare* 44,4,Fall, 12-17.
Survey of all US agencies with child placement responsibilities shows almost all states as having policies relating to children in foster family care but wide variation as to the content of these policies and no consensus on standards regarding visiting.

193 *HOREJSI CR, BERTSCHE AV & CLARK FW (1981) *Social work practice with parents of children in foster care* Illinois: Charles C Thomas. 241pp.
In the same question-and-answer format as HOREJSI's *Foster family care* (162), this publication is derived from a demonstration training project in Montana and is intended for inexperienced practitioners. Sections on parents and the importance of parental visiting; and working with parents, including service agreements/ contracts and the use of informal helping resources.

194 *HUGHES P (1984) 'Access and parental rights resolutions: the changes' *Adoption & Fostering* 8,3, 18-21.
Changes in legislation discussed from a legal perspective.

195 JENKINS S & NORMAN E (1972) *Filial deprivation and foster care* NY: Columbia University Press. 296pp.
Part of the Columbia longitudinal study, a five-year follow-up of children entering foster care in New York City in 1966. Useful findings on the ambivalence and complexity of parental reactions to the loss of their children, including feelings of 'filial deprivation'. Results emphasise the need for urgent and intensive action if children are to be restored to their families.

196 JENKINS S & NORMAN E (1975) *Beyond placement: mothers view foster care* NY: Columbia University Press. 149pp
Further material from the above study includes consumer reactions from mothers. Authors call for a 'no-fault' foster care system available to all as needed and characterised by a family-focused approach, minimal stigma, and a recognition of the social and economic pressures on families.

197 *JOHNSON D (1986) 'Access: the natural family's dilemma' *Adoption & Fostering* 10,3, 42-46.
Criticises the negative view which many social workers adopt towards parental access and discusses ways in which positive access may be facilitated.

198 KELLY G (1981) 'The lost cord' *Social Work Today* 13, 12, 24 Nov, 7-9.
Brief review of research findings on parental contact for children in care, highlighting the discrepancy between research demonstrating the value of contact and the practice reality of little actual contact.

199 KELLY G (1985) 'Family contact: a study in Northern Ireland' *Adoption & Fostering* 9,4, 52-56.
Belfast study of parent-child contact which goes against the trend of previous research in that parents are able to sustain contact. The sample contained a high proportion of siblings and legitimate children. Author speculates that contact may be better as the community is generally more cohesive.

200 LITTNER N (1975) 'The importance of the natural parents to the child in placement' *Child Welfare* 54,3,March, 175-181.
Recognising the considerable difficulties which birth parents may present to foster parents, the author argues strongly for foster parent understanding towards the birth parent, for the benefit of the child.

201 MALUCCIO AN & SINANOGLU PA (1981) 'Social work with parents of children in foster care: a bibliography' *Child Welfare* 60,5,May, 275-303.
Helpful compilation of almost 400 references, mainly 1970-1980.

202 **MARSH P (1986) 'Natural families and children in care: an agenda for practice development' *Adoption & Fostering* 10,4, 20-25 & 19.
Paper on the practice implications of recent findings about the lack of involvement of families in the lives of their children in care.

203 MECH EV (1985) 'Parental visiting and foster placement' *Child Welfare* 64,1,Jan/Feb, 67-72.
US national survey of over 1500 children in care confirms the importance of parental visiting for reducing time in foster care, but emphasises that 'visiting' is a complex issue.

204 *MILLHAM S, BULLOCK R, HOSIE K & LITTLE M (1985) 'Maintaining family links of children in care' *Adoption and Fostering* 9,2, 12-16.
Summary of the research findings published in 045.

205 MILNER JL (1987) 'An ecological perspective on duration of foster care' *Child Welfare* 66, 2, Mar/Apr, 113-123.
Study of 75 children in care of Alabama agency, discharged from care during previous 14 months. Strong statistical relationship between child's relationship with own family during placement and duration of placement: frequent, positive parental visiting associated with shorter placements. Agency responsiveness to family also very important: intense social work activity with family associated with early discharge from care.

206 POULIN JE (1985) 'Long term foster care, natural family attachment and loyalty conflict' *Journal of Social Service Research* 9,1,Fall, 17-29.
Study of 80 foster children found that those who were most adversely affected by their long-term foster care status were those who were psychologically attached to their natural families. Continuing contact strengthens this attachment, making their placement in foster care more difficult for them to accept. Author warns of need to examine further factors.

207   PROCH K & HOWARD JA (1986) 'Parental visiting of children in
foster care' Social Work 31,3,May/June, 178-181.
Illinois study of 256 children. For 70% a visiting plan for parents was explicit or
implicit. No relationship was noted between frequency of visits planned and age of
child. Most parents scheduled to visit did so within the terms of the schedule.
Where there was no schedule, or where parents were told to ask for a visit when
they wanted one, parents did not visit. Visiting plans were seldom individualised
and bore little relationship to the needs of child or family, but more to worker's style
and standard practices in the agency. There was little social worker involvement in
visits.

208   **SINANOGLU P & MALUCCIO AN (eds)(1981) Parents of
children in placement: perspectives and programs NY: Child Welfare
League of America. 475pp.
Very useful collection of 30 papers, some especially written for this publication,
others – such as those by COLON (185), Fanshel, Goldstein, Jenkins, LITTNER
(200), and Stein et al – previously published in a variety of journals and already
beginning to achieve 'classic' status.

209   TIDDY SG (1986) 'Creative co-operation: involving biological
parents in long-term foster care' Child Welfare 65,1,Jan/Feb, 53-62.
Author advocates going beyong 'contact' to the real involvement of parents in the
lives of their children in care.

210   TUNNARD J (ed)(1982) Fostering parental contact: arguments in
favour of preserving contact between children in care and their families
Family Rights Group. 75pp.
Papers by Robin Benians (on psychiatric issues), Jennifer Levin (legal), Elizabeth
Woodman (on access), Robert Holman (inclusive and exclusive care), Liz Ratcliffe
(a foster parent), and Mary Reistroffer. Also parents' accounts of their experiences.

FOSTER PARENTS

Much of the ambiguity in foster care noted earlier centres on the role of
foster parents in relation to foster children, birth parents and agencies.
STEVENSON offers an excellent introduction to fostering, addressed
primarily to foster parents but recommendable to anyone with an interest
in the subject. The study by GEORGE gives a good deal of attention to the
self-perceptions of 'traditional' foster parents and the author's recommendations point ahead to the more 'professional' role currently being
developed, particularly in specialist fostering (see also FULLERTON).
EASTMAN provides a useful analysis of the foster family and its

ambiguities in terms of systems theory. The study undertaken by CAUTLEY of the experiences of a group of foster parents through their first 18 months repays careful study, not least for its emphasis on the importance of that neglected figure, the foster father.

211   ADAMSON G (1973) *The caretakers* Bookstall Publications. 276pp.
Study undertaken in the 1960s of foster parents' experiences and attitudes.

212   BERMAN LC (1986) 'Foster parents as a resource in preparing children with developmental disabilities for placement' *Adoption & Fostering* 10,2, 40-43.
Foster parents are in a key position to prepare children for a move, but account needs to be taken of foster parents' feelings of anger, sadness and grief. Social work support is needed so that foster parents can give child permission to become attached to new family.

213   CARBINO R (1980) *Foster parenting: an updated review of the literature* NY: Child Welfare League of America. 43pp.
Review of US research studies, mainly from the 1970s.

214   *CAUTLEY PW (1980) *New foster parents: the first experience* NY: Human Sciences Press. 287pp.
US study following foster parents through their first 18 months and suggesting some indicators of successful fostering, including familiarity with children, good parenting models from childhood, willingness to work with social worker and agency, and verbal evidence of parenting skills as applied to specific behaviour incidents. Foster fathers emerged as particularly important in determining the likely success of the placement.

215   DAVIDS L (1973) 'Foster fatherhood: the untapped resource' *Child Welfare* 52,2,Feb, 100-108.
Includes brief account of a small-scale study showing the need to define more clearly the role of foster father and include him more constructively in foster care planning.

216   *EASTMAN K (1979) 'The foster family in a systems theory perspective' *Child Welfare* 58,9,Nov, 564-570.
Application of systems thinking to the foster home throws light on some of the stresses experienced by foster families, relating to lack of role clarity and uncertainty as to boundaries. Too much change as well as too much openness can be detrimental to the system's wellbeing and sense of identity. The foster home has a vague identity: "just as a foster child may have a hard time knowing to whom he belongs, the foster family may have a hard time knowing who belongs to it".

217   EDELSTEIN S (1981) 'When foster children leave: helping foster parents to grieve' *Child Welfare* 60,7,July/August, 467-473.
Relating theory of grief and its resolution to the situation of foster parents. Importance of honest communication, relationship with social worker, training, self-help groups, and supportive legislation.

218   *FULLERTON M (1982) 'A study of the role of foster parents in family placement for adolescents' *Clearing House for Local Authority Social Services Research* 4, 45-138. University of Birmingham Department of Social Administration.
Comparative study of two small groups of foster parents – 'traditional' and 'professional' – suggesting that the latter gained more satisfaction from a sense of carrying out a professional task and looked less for responsiveness and emotional gratification from the child.

219   HAMPSON RB & TAVORMINA JB (1980) 'Feedback from the experts: a study of foster mothers' *Social Work* 25,2, March, 108-113.
Results of interviews with 34 foster mothers in Virginia on their motives, the rewards and problems of fostering, attitudes to discipline, with discussion of issues arising.

220   JONES E (1986) *Two worlds* Social Care Association/NFCA, 87pp.
Story of a foster child by her foster mother.

221   JONES EO (1975) 'A study of those who cease to foster' *British Journal of Social Work* 5,1, 31-41.
Portsmouth study of ex-foster parents shows considerable confusion about the foster parent role and the foster parent-social worker relationship, and concludes that there is little to be gained from higher recruitment while there is a lack of support for those already engaged in fostering. (That a substantial number of those interviewed were unaware of their 'ex'-status is in itself a comment on agency-foster parent communication.) Forty per cent had ceased to foster after less than a year. One notable finding was that many ex-foster fathers had not been positively motivated or closely involved.

222   LITTNER N (1978) 'The art of being a foster parent' *Child Welfare* 57,1, Jan, 3-12.
Neatly itemises the pressures on foster parents from various sources, fully justifying the understated conclusion that "it is not easy to be a foster parent".

223   MEEZAN W & SHIREMAN JF (1982) 'Foster parent adoption: a literature review' *Child Welfare* 61,8, Nov/Dec, 525-535.
Review of research and practice literature relevant to situations where foster homes turn into adoptive homes.

224   MEEZAN W & SHIREMAN JF (1985) *Care and commitment: foster parent adoption decisions* NY: State University. 247pp.
Chicago study involving 95 children to discover the differences between foster parents who chose to adopt their foster children and those who did not. Interesting incidental finding that the foster/adoptive parents were better at predicting placement outcome than were the social workers.

225   MILLER B (1986) *Room for one more: surviving as a foster mum* John Murray with NFCA. 128pp.
Account of the experiences of a foster mother, by one of the survivors.

226   **NATIONAL FOSTER CARE ASSOCIATION *Adoption – you and your foster child / Caring and sharing is fostering / Caring for a foster child under five / Case conferences and reviews / Coping with a fostering breakdown / Coping with court: a guide for foster parents / Custodianship – you and your foster child (England and Wales) / Custody – you and your foster child (Scotland) / Foster care allowances and income tax / Household insurance for foster parents / If your foster child is charged with an offence (England and Wales) / Integrating the foster child into the family / Making good use of a social worker's visit / Questions and answers about fostering / Role of the child's parents in foster care / Thinking of fostering a teenager?* NFCA.
One of NFCA's very practical contributions to fostering is its steadily expanding series of pamphlets and leaflets providing basic information in handy short form. Addressed primarily to foster parents but helpful to anyone interested in the topics.

227   PROCH K (1981) 'Foster parents as preferred adoptive parents: practice implications' *Child Welfare* 60,9,Nov, 617-625.
US questionnaire study of agency policies regarding preference given to foster parents as adopters of their foster children. (Are there implications here for custodianship and adoption in the UK?)

228   ROCHE E & DUNNE A (1986) *Children in long-term foster care: the impact of the placement upon twenty foster families* Barnardo's North East Division. 32pp.
Exploratory and descriptive study of foster parents' reactions to various stages of foster care, from assessment to the impact of the placement on the foster family.

229   ROWE J, CAIN H, HUNDLEBY M & KEANE A (1984) *Long-term fostering and the Children Act: a study of foster parents who went on to adopt* BAAF. 34pp.
Substudy derived from ROWE *et al* 1984 (see 178). Some interesting findings, including the point that an adoption order did not seem to make much difference to natural parent-child contact: in most cases it had either ceased long before or else continued despite the adoption. Also social workers considered those foster parents who adopted to be more likely than those who did not adopt to be open with the child about background information.

230   SHAW M (1986) 'Substitute parenting' in W Sluckin & M Herbert (eds) *Parental behaviour* Basil Blackwell, 259-282.
Review of US and UK research literature on parenting behaviour in foster and adoptive parents, including such topics as characteristics and motivation of foster parents; attitudes and behaviour; foster parents and children as consumers; and, in adoption, childlessness and role handicap, the question of origins and parenting 'hard-to-place' children.

231   SHAW M & LEBENS K (1977) 'Foster parents talking' *Adoption & Fostering* 1,2, 11-16.
Research interviews with 44 long-term foster parents on the satisfactions and frustrations of fostering, the latter stemming from natural parents and the agency rather than the children. 'Exclusive' care emerged as the dominant model.

232   **STEVENSON O (1977) *Someone else's child: a book for foster parents of young children* Routledge & Kegan Paul. 122pp.
Helpful, non-technical discussion of questions arising in the care of other people's children.

233   TRASLER G (1960) *In place of parents: a study of foster care* Routledge & Kegan Paul. 248pp.
Study of foster parents in which the author laid particular emphasis on careful attention to their expectations of the foster child as an indicator of likely success or failure.

234   WILKES JR (1974) 'The impact of fostering on the foster family' *Child Welfare* 53,6,June, 373-379.
Discussion of a somewhat neglected aspect of foster family care, focusing on four sources of stress: disruption of the family equilibrium; coping with the child in transition; dealing with the 'alien agency'; and harbouring 'great expectations'.

Foster parent recruitment, selection and training

The period under review shows a marked shift in the approach adopted by agencies towards prospective foster parents, from one characterised by detailed scrutiny of their personal history, attitudes and motives, to a more open, educational approach addressed to tasks and skills. The NFCA material lays considerable emphasis on the process as well as the content of foster parent training, including the use of existing foster parents as co-trainers in their courses. The emphasis on how to train foster parents as much as on what they need to know is reflected in most recent literature.

235 *ANDERSON LM (1982) 'A systems theory model for foster home studies' *Child Welfare* 61, 1, Jan, 37-47.
Discussion of the application of systems and communication theories to foster home assessment and 'matching'. Theories outlined and illustrated by practice examples.

236 BIRCHALL D (1983) 'Foster parents, their recruitment, selection and training: a review of recent research findings' National Children's Bureau *Highlight* no. 56. 2pp.
Brief note on 22 studies published between 1975 and 1982.

237 DARE R (1984) 'Know thyself' *Community Care* 2 August, 18-20.
Consultant psychologist looks at the effect of a foster child on the foster family and concludes that the social worker's job is to help the family understand how their own needs relate to those of the child.

238 *DAVIS S, MORRIS B & THORN J (1984) 'Task-centred assessment for foster parents' *Adoption & Fostering* 8,4, 33-37.
Discussion of the use of a task-centred approach to foster parent selection as an alternative to a psychodynamic, history-taking model.

239 ENGEL JM (1983) 'The parent therapist program: a new approach to foster care of difficult adolescents' *Children & Youth Services Review* 5, 195-207.
Account of a training programme for specialist foster parents, with a preliminary evaluation of its effectiveness.

240   FREELING NW, KISSEL S & SURGENT L (1976) 'Parenting for foster parents' *Child Psychiatry & Human Development* 6, 4, summer, 244-250.
Describes a parenting course for foster parents: learning theory principles and techniques, communication skills, conflict resolution, child development, information of community services. Evaluation suggests participants found the course helpful and were using the knowledge acquired.

241   FREUND VW (1976) 'Evaluation of a self-approval method for inducting foster parents' *Smith College Studies in Social Work* 46, March, 114-126.
New Jersey foster parent training course in which staff sought to share with applicants the responsibility for deciding whether or not to foster. Two-thirds dropped out of the course, some still had to be counselled out, others were 'accepted' but decision made not to use them. Positive feedback from those who stayed the course. Staff uncertainties about not really 'knowing' the families were also overcome.

242   GUERNEY L (1977) 'A description and evaluation of a skills training program for foster parents' *American Journal of Community Psychology* 5, 3, 361-371.
Comparative study of a training and non-training group. The former subsequently showed greater improvement in accepting attitudes towards the children; also greater ability to employ 'desirable' and to refrain from 'undesirable' parental responses.

243   GUERNEY LF & GAVIGAN MA (1981) 'Parental acceptance and foster parents' *Journal of Clinical Child Psychology*, Winter, 27-32.
Study showing the relevance of the Porter Parental Acceptance scale to work with foster parents. (NB This is about acceptance of children by foster parents, not acceptance of natural parents!)

244   JACOBS M (1980) 'Foster parent training: an opportunity for skills enrichment and empowerment' *Child Welfare* 59, 1, Dec, 615-624.
Model for group training of foster parents focusing on self-directed learning and mutual support to overcome feelings of powerlessness and isolation. Stresses value of seeing adult learner as a full partner in the educational experience.

245   JORDAN A & RODWAY MR (1984) 'Correlates of effective foster parenting' *Social Work Research & Abstracts* 20, 2, summer, 27-31.
Review of research literature showing little success in attempts to relate psychological variables and motivation to subsequent performance. Heimler Scale of Social Functioning shows more interesting possibilities in distinguishing more from less effective foster parents in Alberta.

246   KAY N (1966) 'A systematic approach to selecting foster parents' *Case Conference* 13,2,June; also reprinted in R Tod (ed)(1971) *Social work in foster care* Longman, 39-50.

Still frequently-cited article in which the author argues from his own practice experience that, for long-term foster parents, there are two principal motivations, at least one of which must be present if the placement is to survive the normal stresses and strains: (1) applicants urgently desire a child or further child of their own but are unable or unwilling to conceive one; (2) applicants identify strongly with deprived or unhappy children because of memories of deprivation or unhappiness in their own childhood.

247   McWHINNIE AM (1979) 'Foster parents study' paper presented at *First International Conference on Foster Care*, 58-70. NFCA.

Small study seeking to identify common factors in a group of foster parents 'preferred' by social workers. As well as a number of typically middle-class characteristics, 'surplus energy' emerged as important for success.

248   NATIONAL FOSTER CARE ASSOCIATION (1977) *Education and training in foster care: a report with recommendations* NFCA. 60pp.

249   *NATIONAL FOSTER CARE ASSOCIATION (1980) *Introduction to foster parenting - parenting plus* NFCA.

250   *NATIONAL FOSTER CARE ASSOCIATION (1982) *Added to adolescence - foster parenting an adolescent* NFCA.

251   NATIONAL FOSTER CARE ASSOCIATION (1983) *Foster care education project: looking back – looking forward* NFCA. 105pp.

Widely used and very successful foster care training packs, modified for UK use from material originally devised by the Child Welfare League of America. The 1983 publication is an evaluation of the training courses in which these packs were used.

252   PENN JV (1978) 'A model for training foster parents in behavior modification techniques' *Child Welfare* 57,3,March, 175-180.

Account of a group training programme and the positive outcome in relation to the children placed with the foster families. (Incidentally emphasises the possible damaging effects of a foster home breakdown on the foster parents' own children.)

253   ROWE DC (1976) 'Attitudes, social class and the quality of foster care' *Social Service Review* 50,3,Sept, 506-514.

Study suggesting that the social class of the foster parent is unrelated to the quality of foster care, though the researcher warns of possible bias in his methodology.

254   SOOTHILL K (1980) 'Recruitment campaigns' *Adoption & Fostering* 4,1, 52-58.

255   SOOTHILL K & DERBYSHIRE M (1981) 'Selecting foster parents' *Adoption & Fostering* 5,2, 47-50 & 64.

256   SOOTHILL K & DERBYSHIRE M (1982) 'Retention of foster parents' *Adoption & Fostering* 6,2, 38-43.
Evaluative study of a foster parent campaign in Lancashire.

257   WIEHE VR (1982) 'Differential personality types of foster parents' *Social Work Research & Abstracts* 18,2, 16-20.
Study of 218 foster parents revealed differences in personality type between foster fathers and foster mothers which may have implications for training and for subsequent relationships with social workers.

258   WIEHE VR (1983) 'Foster mothers: are they unique?' *Psychological Reports* 53, 1215-1218.
Briefly, yes! Postal questionnaire responses showed foster mothers scored significantly higher than non-foster mothers on the 'social' and lower on the 'enterprising' scale. Younger foster mothers differed from older ones in attaining higher scores on the 'realistic', 'social', 'enterprising' and 'artistic' scales. Author suggests younger foster mothers take a more assertive approach in their role, which may be helpful in making changes necessary in the foster care system.

FOSTER CHILDREN

"No one ever asked us ..." is the plaintive cry taken as the title for FESTINGER's study of foster children. Well, some researchers are beginning to ask (eg BUSH *et al*, REST & WATSON, THORPE, TRISELIOTIS and WITTNER) and it is to be hoped that foster children's views will help to shape future policy and practice. As will be seen later in this section, most interest now centres on children who are, for a variety of reasons, deemed 'hard to place'.

259   **BUSH M, GORDON AC & LeBAILLY R (1977) 'Evaluating child welfare services: a contribution from the clients' *Social Service Review* 51, 3, Sept, 491-501.
Illinois study of children aged 10-18 in foster care. The authors point to the simplicity of the children's wishes (love, care and understanding) and warn against searching for more professional-sounding, quasi-scientific criteria for foster parents.

260 *FANSHEL D & SHINN EB (1978) *Children in foster care: a longitudinal investigation* NY: Columbia University Press. 520pp.
This is a large-scale, detailed study of over 600 New York City children who first came into care between 1966 and 1971. Particularly striking finding is the significance of parent-child contact for rehabilitation and for the children's well-being in care.

261 FESTINGER T (1983) *No one ever asked us . . . a postscript to foster care* NY: Columbia University Press. 343pp.
Interview study of 277 young adults discharged from foster care in New York in 1975 who had spent at least the preceding five years in care and who were aged 18-21 years at discharge.

262 FRANK G (1980) 'Treatment needs of children in foster care' *American Journal of Orthopsychiatry* 50, 2, April, 256-263.
Substudy of 50 children (linked to 261, NY Columbia review of children in care) looking at psychosocial problems at the beginning and end of the five-year period. 80% of children found to be seriously in need of treatment at the start, and general deterioration noted by the end. The author suggests that "foster care services may thus be largely geographic, that is a change in address rather than in quality of care".

263 KAVANAGH S (1986) 'Too much understanding in foster homes?' *Adoption & Fostering* 10, 3, 19-23.
The writer, who is a foster parent and psychologist, offers a case-study as a basis for her argument that there has been too much emphasis on 'understanding' and too little on setting limits which prepare children for the realities of adult life.

264 LAWDER EA, POULIN JE & ANDREWS RG (1986) 'A study of 185 foster children five years after placement' *Child Welfare* 65, 3, May/June, 241-251.
Follow-up study (from case records) after five years of children placed in foster care by Children's Aid Society of Pennsylvania during a six-month period in 1979. No follow-up data on those discharged early. 62% had returned home, 16% adopted, 18% still in care. Strongest predictor was frequency of child's contact with own family. Children in care for reasons of neglect, children with most behaviour problems, of teenage parents, or of parents with mental health problems stayed in care longest.

265 O'CONNELL M (1976) *Helping the child to use foster family care* ABAFA. 20pp.
Pamphlet dealing with help given to a child through work with the parents, foster parents and directly to the foster child, with particular attention to identity problems.

266   POWLEY P (1985) 'Family preparation group for children' *Adoption & Fostering* 9, 1, 41-44.
Descriptive account of a group for children aged six to ten years in which emphasis was placed on looking ahead to foster family life.

267   REST ER & WATSON KW (1984) 'Growing up in foster care' *Child Welfare* 63, 4, July/Aug, 291-306.
Survey of a small sample of adults fostered as children suggests that 'impermanence' did not impair their ability to lead independent, outwardly satisfactory lives, but left them at risk of an impaired self-image from the deeply felt stigma of foster care, difficulty in establishing emotional intimacy, and an unresolved sense of loss.

268   SHAPIRO D (1976) *Agencies and foster children* NY:Columbia University Press. 216pp.
Research study of the impact over a five-year period of agency investment in the New York City child welfare system. Over 80 agencies studied. Evidence of impact during first two year period but falling off thereafter, resulting in drift. Black children more likely to remain within the system.

269   **THORPE R (1980) 'The experiences of children and parents living apart: implications and guidelines for practice' in J TRISELIOTIS (ed) (see 182).
English study replicating WEINSTEIN 1960 (see 271) on the amount and quality of parent-child contact.

270   *TRISELIOTIS J (1980) 'Growing up in foster care and after' in J TRISELIOTIS (ed) (see 182).
Study of 40 young people in Scotland who had spent 7-15 years each in a single foster home before the age of sixteen. Author derived four categories of foster parent-child relationship: *mutually satisfying, possessive, professional, ambivalent*. Notes generally a tendency to low aspirations by and of foster children: "setting low sights and expectations appears to be endemic to foster child placement in contrast to adoption".

271   WEINSTEIN EA (1960) *The self-image of the foster child* NY: Russell Sage Foundation. 80pp.
Classic influential study seeking to demonstrate the importance of parental contact for the wellbeing of children in care.

272   WITTNER JG (1981) 'Entering foster care: foster children's accounts' *Children & Youth Services Review* 3, 21-35.
Research interviews with 43 young people aged 14-21 years who had spent at least two years in foster care, in more than one placement. Uses C Wright Mills' concept of 'vocabularies of motives'.

273   WOLKIND S & RUTTER M (1973) 'Children who have been in care - an epidemiological study' *Child Psychology & Psychiatry* 14, 2, 97-105. Study of ten and eleven year olds showing a strong association in boys between antisocial behaviour and a history which includes a short period in foster home or residential care. The study took place years after the care period and most of the children who had been in care were found to be living in large families characterised by parental discord. Authors suggest that it is the long-term family disturbance which leads to the emotional disorder rather than the short time in care *per se*. The findings suggest the need for preventive treatment for families seeking short-term admission to care for their children.

CHILDREN WHO ARE 'HARD TO PLACE'

There is considerable overlap between adoption and foster family care in the literature on children who are 'hard to place' (sometimes referred to as children with 'special needs') and it is advisable to consult the corresponding headings (403-452) under ADOPTION when seeking material on any particular 'category' of children. Children are generally considered hard to place on grounds of age, medical condition or handicap (with or without accompanying behaviour problems), being part of a sibling group, or by reason of ethnic origin. (The latter children are considered in the ETHNIC ISSUES IN CHILD WELFARE section, 469-511.) To these categories should now be added children who have been sexually abused.

Older children

The fostering of older children in this country largely originated with the work of Nancy Hazel and her colleagues in Kent, and her book provides an excellent introduction to the thinking that went into their pioneer scheme (HAZEL 1981). A broader review of the development of specialist fostering in the UK and the issues faced by specialist schemes is to be found in SHAW & HIPGRAVE. The papers by DOWNES and DOWNES & HALL look at some of the hard practicalities of time-limited fostering for teenagers. The forthcoming collection of papers edited by ALDGATE *et al* should offer an up-to-date picture of the 'state of the art'. See also HOGHUGHI & HIPGRAVE (159).

274   *ALDGATE J, MALUCCIO AN & REEVES C (eds) (1988) *Aolescents in foster family placements* Batsford/BAAF.
Collection of original papers on various aspects of the placement of teenagers in foster family care.

275   BRYANT B (1981) 'Special foster care: a history and rationale' *Journal of Clinical Child Psychology* 10, 1, Winter, 8-20.
Detailed account of the development of specialist fostering in the US and discussion of policy and practice issues.

276   *DOWNES C (1982) 'How endings are experienced in time-limited family placement of difficult adolescents' *Journal of Adolescence* 5, Dec, 379-394.
From a preliminary study of placements in the Bradford Community Parents Project the author identifies four patterns of reaction by teenagers and their foster parents to the prospect of the placement coming to an end, and discusses the implications for practice.

277   *DOWNES C (1982) 'Assessing adolescents for time-limited foster care' *Adoption & Fostering* 6, 4, 26-30 & 53.
Related to the above study, this paper emphasises the importance for the adolescent of being seen in the context of existing attachments, and being given the opportunity to find and use adults outside the formal caring network.

278   *DOWNES C & HALL S (1982) 'Success and failure in fostering' *Foster Care* March, 4-6.
Discussion of some of the complexities involved in seeking to understand and assess the needs of difficult adolescents and to find ways of meeting these within a foster family placement.

279   **HAZEL N (1981) *A bridge to independence* Basil Blackwell. 175pp.
Account of the pioneer Kent Family Placement Scheme which was to become the model for most specialist schemes throughout the UK.

280   KENT FAMILY PLACEMENT SERVICE (1985) *Ten years on – a pioneer teenage fostering scheme* Kent County Council Social Services Department. 57pp.
Account of the history, development and progress of the Kent scheme, with contributions from social workers, foster parents and others currently involved.

281   NATIONAL FOSTER CARE ASSOCIATION (1985) *Teenagers in care – seminars on fostering adolescents* NFCA. 73pp.
Seminar papers on teenage fostering by Terry Barrett, Tony Hipgrave, Derek Raffaelli, Martin Shaw and Helen Taylor, plus material from workshops on related topics.

282 *SHAW M & HIPGRAVE T (1983) *Specialist fostering* Batsford/
BAAF. 152pp.
Account of two research studies – the first a detailed study of an adolescent
fostering scheme in one local authority, the second a questionnaire survey of
specialist schemes throughout the country – followed by discussion of policy and
practice issues to be faced in specialist fostering.

283 SMITH PM (1986) 'Evaluation of Kent placements' *Adoption &
Fostering* 10, 1, 29-33.
Evaluation of 92 completed placements in the Kent Family Placement Scheme
January 1984 to June 1985.

284 TIMBERLAKE EM & VERIECK MJ (1987) 'Psychosocial functioning
of adolescents in foster care' *Social Casework* 68, 4, April, 214-222.
US agency study of 71 adolescents in foster care, using information provided by the
foster parents. The practice implications of the findings, an 'asset' profile and a
'vulnerability' profile are discussed.

285 TOZER R (1979) 'Treatment fostering' *Adoption & Fostering* 3, 1, 26-
33.
Descriptive account of several North American pioneer schemes for the 'treatment'
fostering of adolescents.

Sexually abused children

Perhaps what will date this publication more precisely than anything else is
the fact that it contains just three references on children who have been
sexually abused. As happens from time to time in social work, practice is
here well ahead of the literature, and there is clearly an enormous need for
material to assist those involved in this highly complex area of family
placement.

286 NATIONAL FOSTER CARE ASSOCIATION (1987) *Fostering a
sexually abused child* NFCA. 12pp.
Helpful pamphlet providing information and advice for foster parents.

287 ROBERTS J (1986) 'Fostering the sexually abused child' *Adoption &
Fostering* 10, 1, 8-11.
Guidance for foster parents on the care of sexually abused children, derived from
writer's practice in Lambeth unit.

288   SMITH G (1986) 'Child sexual abuse: the power of intrusion'
Adoption & Fostering 10,3, 13-18.
Article on sexual abuse followed by contribution from a foster parent with the care
of a sexually abused child.

Children with medical conditions and handicaps

BARNARDO'S have been pioneers in this field and the book by DIXON *et*
al charts the progress of their scheme since its inception. There is also
much to be learned from the adoption literature on this topic, for example
MACASKILL and WEDGE & THOBURN. As is the case with sexual
abuse, there are gaps to be filled in the next few years on family placement
for children suffering from AIDS.

289   *BAAF (1987) *Implications of AIDS for children in care* BAAF. 84pp.
Papers on paediatric, legal and social work aspects.

290   BARNARDO'S NEW FAMILIES PROJECT (1983) *Bridge families*
scheme Colchester: Barnardo's New Families Project. 42pp.
Account of scheme to give children a 'bridging' experience, eg for severely
institutionalised children, experience of family life prior to permanent family
placement; for older children, experience of family life prior to leaving care; respite
care for children with physical or mental handicaps; and temporary care for
children who have experienced the breakdown of a 'permanent' placement.

291   BRITISH INSTITUTE OF MENTAL HANDICAP (1980) *Family*
placements for mentally handicapped children: report of a residential
workshop BIMH. 66pp.
Report of a workshop which examined a number of issues: bringing up children
with disabilities; children with handicaps in the family; behavioural aspects and
behaviour problems; special needs of children with multiple handicaps; finding
parents for children with severe handicaps; and recruitment methods.

292   *CURTIS S (ed)(1987) *From asthma to thalassaemia: medical*
conditions in childhood BAAF. 159pp.
Information on a wide range of conditions and their implications for the care of
children who are affected.

293   *DIXON N, FLANAGAN R, HARDY J, KERMODE S, DODSON L
& SPENCER C (1987) *Special fostering: fostering children and young*
people who are mentally handicapped Barnardo Practice Papers. 113pp.
Report on a Barnardo project set up in 1979 to find foster homes for children and
young people with mental disabilities. Each stage of the process is evaluated, and
feedback from foster parents is included.

294   GATH A (1983) 'Mentally retarded children in substitute and natural families' *Adoption & Fostering* 7, 1, 35-40.
Study of children with Down's syndrome or other mental handicap placed in foster and adoptive homes.

295   GURDIN P & ANDERSON GR (1987) 'Quality care for ill children: AIDS-specialized foster family homes' *Child Welfare* 66, 4, July/August, 291-302.
Account of a New York City project to recruit families for children suffering from AIDS. Recruitment proved difficult and was achieved through the existing foster parent network rather than by large-scale publicity. Common factors in the six foster families recruited were *knowledge* about AIDS, *confidence* that they were not endangering themselves or other family members, *medical training* and a *history of illness*, notably cancer in themselves or in a close relative.

296   HART G (1987) 'Placing children with AIDS' *Adoption & Fostering* 11, 1, 41-43.
Brief discussion of AIDS and the implications for agencies and for substitute families.

297   KEEFE A (1983) *Foster care: a research study on the NCH Foster Care Project in Gloucester and Avon* Harpenden: National Children's Home. 60pp.
Independent evaluation of a three year pilot programme, describing the recruitment methods used and the results. Placements of children with mental handicaps were an unqualified success, the placements of other children less so.

298   *NATIONAL FOSTER CARE ASSOCIATION (1987) *AIDS and HIV – information for foster parents* NFCA. 10pp.
Brief introduction to the subject for foster parents.

Siblings

With the rapid rundown of residential provision, finding foster or adoptive homes for sibling groups has become a matter of serious concern to many agencies. To split or not to split? How can contact best be maintained between brothers and sisters placed in different families? Such questions have as yet received surprisingly little attention in the literature. (See also 450-452.)

299   ALDRIDGE MJ & CAUTLEY PW (1976) 'Placing siblings in the same foster home' *Child Welfare* 55, 2, Feb, 85-93.
Study of 115 placements suggests that placing siblings together is neither a guarantee of success nor predictive of lack of success. Placing siblings together does not necessarily undermine the placement. Workers were more likely to place less disturbed children and those with fewest previous placements with their siblings, which in itself will influence outcome. It was found that the *birth* family was more likely to be a disruptive influence when siblings were placed together.

300   MORRISON T & BROWN J (1986) 'Splitting siblings' *Adoption & Fostering* 10, 4, 47-51.
Case-study involving the separate placement of three siblings.

301   TIMBERLAKE EM & HAMLIN ER (1982) 'The sibling group: a neglected dimension of placement' *Child Welfare* 61, 8, Nov/Dec, 545-552.
Discussion of practice issues, mainly on handling the situation where only one member of a sibling group is to be placed in care.

302   WARD M (1984) 'Sibling ties in foster care and adoption planning' *Child Welfare* 63 ,4, July/Aug, 321-332.
Discussion of the importance of sibling ties, with recommendations for maintaining links throughout the placement process.

3   Adoption

GENERAL

The area of child welfare which has seen the greatest changes in thinking, policy and practice since around 1970 is undoubtedly adoption. The developments which precipitated these changes have been well chronicled: the sharp reduction in the numbers of healthy, white babies being offered for adoption, thanks to improvements in contraception, the greater availability of abortion, and somewhat greater social tolerance of single parenthood; and the increased awareness of children 'drifting' in care, subjected to all-too-frequent changes of placement, social worker and agency policy. The recognition that 'permanency' could not readily be achieved within the care system put increasing pressure on adoption services to provide family life for children who for whatever reason could not be returned to their families of origin. Within a remarkably short space of time, adoption agencies (or those which survived the revolution, at least) switched their aspirations from 'the perfect baby for the perfect family' to 'a family for every child, not a child for the childless family'.

The impact of these changes on adoption literature can be clearly seen when surveying material from the 1950s and 1960s as compared with the 1970s and 1980s. Broadly speaking, literature of the earlier period focused on work with young unmarried mothers (occasionally fathers), the timing and appropriateness of their consent to adoption, the care and assessment of their babies as to their suitability for adoption, the quest for the ideal adoptive couple, and the careful 'matching' of baby and adoptive applicants. From 1970 onwards, it becomes increasingly difficult to find new material on the assessment of birth parents, babies or adopters: parents in the literature are characteristically older, the children are also older and often with mental or physical handicap or behavioural disorder; and there are no longer clear rules as to who is or is not 'suitable' to adopt these children, not even on such crude indicators as age, religion, marital or economic status, or fertility.

The switch from illegitimate babies to older children with an identifiable family of origin and some sense of their own history has raised questions as to the appropriateness of the secrecy of traditional adoption practice – the new name and birth certificate, the closing (in US parlance, the sealing) of the original birth records, the cutting of all links with the family origin, and other such measures intended to give the child a 'fresh start'. Since the Children Act 1975 gave adopted people in England and Wales (following the Scottish example) the right to obtain their original birth certificates, there have been some moves towards more openness in adoption. However, there is far from unanimous support for further openness (eg adoption with continuing contact with the birth family), and for that reason the US debate on open adoption is of more than academic interest (PANNOR & BARAN; SORICH & SIEBERT).

The best starting-points in the adoption literature are BEAN for current issues and developments (the coverage being broader than the sub-title suggests), and SMITH in relation to practice.

303 ASSOCIATION OF BRITISH ADOPTION AND FOSTERING AGENCIES (1977) *Child adoption – a selection of articles on adoption theory and practice* ABAFA. 236pp.
Twenty-eight articles published between 1951 and 1976 in Child Adoption, here arranged under four headings: knowledge from research; the adoption experience; medical aspects; law and courts. Useful collection, including Sants' classic paper on genealogical bewilderment in adopted children.

304 BAAF (1985) *Adoption – some questions answered* BAAF.
Basic information leaflet.

305 BAAF (1982) *Private placements (Section 28a of the Children Act 1975)* BAAF.

306 BAAF (1982) *Adoption and fostering panels* BAAF.

307 BAAF (1984) *Adoption panels in England and Wales* BAAF.

308 BAAF (1984) *Medical aspects of the Adoption Agencies Regulations 1983* BAAF.

309 BAAF (1984) *Using the media* BAAF.

310 BAAF (1985) *Medical aspects of the Adoption Agencies (Scotland) Regulations 1984 and the related court rules* BAAF.

311 BAAF (1985) *Using the BAAF medical forms* BAAF.
Practice notes for adoption agencies. On consent to medical treatment see also 016.

312 **BAAF (1986) *Adopting a child* 2nd edition BAAF 44pp.
Basic information on all stages of the adoption process – why people adopt, adoption agency requirements, adopting children with 'special needs', legal procedures – plus names and addresses of adoption agencies throughout the country. Intended primarily for adopters but a good general guide.

313 **BEAN P (ed)(1984) *Adoption: essays in social policy, law and sociology* Tavistock. 313pp.
Eighteen papers on a wide range of issues including older child adoption, causes and treatment of behaviour problems, a review of research on children growing up adopted, the role of voluntary agencies, obtaining birth certificates, subsidised adoption, and a contribution from an adoptive couple. Legal issues include step-parent adoptions, freeing for adoption, and the role of the court. There are also several papers on transracial adoption.

314 BENET MK (1976) *The character of adoption* Jonathan Cape. 237pp.
Offers an historical and cross-cultural perspective on some of the key issues in contemporary Western adoption. Some fascinating material on adoption in other times and places.

315 BERMAN LC & BUFFERD RK (1986) 'Family treatment to address loss in adoptive families' *Social Casework* 67,1,Jan, 3-11.
Starting from the premise that adoptive parents and children both experience losses that are seldom acknowledged and unique to the adoptive situation, the authors examine the perspectives of those involved and explore treatment strategies for helping families uncover and grieve unresolved losses.

316 DUKETTE R (1984) 'Value issues in present-day adoption' *Child Welfare* 63,3, May/June, 233-243.
Author argues that adoption agencies are facing an identity crisis and must adapt. Particular need for greater openness and flexibility.

317 FRUIN D (1980) 'Sources of statistical information on adoption' *Adoption & Fostering* 4,2, 25-36.
Article describing the principal sources of information on adoption in England, with some suggested improvements as to how such information might be collected.

318 GROTH M, BONNARDELL D, DEVIS DA, MARTIN JC & VOUSDEN HE (1987) 'An agency moves towards open adoption of infants' *Child Welfare* 66,3,May/June, 247-257.
An article recounting the 'process, practice and experience' of an agency in Atlanta moving towards openness in its adoption programme. The practice calls for a considerably greater investment of professional time but is being well received by birth and adoptive parents: in 1985, 75% of placements included openness in some form.

319 HEIM A (1983) *Thicker than water? Adoption: its loyalties, pitfalls and joys* Secker & Warburg. 211pp.
Reflections on adoption, partly derived from the author's own experience as an adoptive parent.

320 HILL M & TRISELIOTIS J (1986) 'Adoption allowances in Scotland: four years on' *Adoption & Fostering* 10,4, 11-19.
Preliminary research report suggests adoption allowances are effective in facilitating the adoption of children. Report notes the growing acceptance of the principle of adoption with payment amongst social workers. (See also 336.)

321 HOKSBERGEN RAC (ed)(1986) *Adoption in worldwide perspective: a review of programs, policies and legislation in 14 countries* Lisse: Swets & Zeitlinger. 242pp. Available from Adoption Centre, University of Utrecht, Heidelberglaan 1, Utrecht-Vithof, Holland.
Short papers from adoption experts in Europe, Asia, Australia, North and South America, each reviewing the adoption scene in their own country. Much on intercountry adoption, surprisingly little on 'hard-to-place' children.

322 HOWE D (1987) 'Adoption trends and counter-trends' *Adoption & Fostering* 11,1, 44-46.
Statistical analysis of adoption trends since 1968, with projections for the future.

323 JOSLING JF & LEVY A (1985) *Adoption of children* 10th edition. Longman. 276pp.
Comprehensive and reliable guide to adoption law.

324 KIRK HD (1981) *Adoptive kinship: a modern institution in need of reform* Butterworth. 173pp.
An interesting blend of social science and personal biography in which the writer seeks to broaden the analysis developed in *Shared fate* (see 368) into consideration of adoption as a social institution.

325 KIRK HD & McDANIEL SA (1984) 'Adoption policy in Great Britain and North America' *Journal of Social Policy* 13,1, 75-84.
Critical examination of what adoption law and policies reveal about the social purposes of adoption and the prevailing values concerning the family – the authors prefer 'shared fate' values to those of Walton family nostalgia!

326 MASSON J, NORBURY D & CHATTERTON SG (1983) *Mine, yours or ours? a study of step-parent adoption* DHSS. 130pp.
Study of step-parent adoptions in three local authority areas, revealing substantial variations in legal and social work practices.

327   MECH EV (1973) 'Adoption: a policy perspective' in BM Caldwell & HN Ricciuti (eds) *Child development and social policy: review of child development research* vol 3 pp. 467-508. Chicago: University of Chicago Press.
Substantial review of adoption research and discussion of policy implications.

328   MOLLAN C & LEFROY L (1985) *New families: your questions on fostering and adoption answered* Turoe Press. 168pp.
Guide to adoption and fostering in the Republic of Ireland, with a question-and-answer section, discussion of issues and a directory of relevant agencies.

329   OXTOBY M (ed) (1981) *Medical practice in adoption and fostering: an introduction* BAAF. 47pp.
Papers on adoption today; guidelines on confidentiality; the role of medical adviser to an adoption agency; and appendices on legal requirements for medical reports, BAAF medical social report forms, and further reading.

330   PANNOR R & BARAN A (1983) 'Open adoption as standard practice' *Child Welfare* 63,3,May/June, 245-250.
In advocating an end to 'closed' adoption, the authors move from their earlier position that openness should be considered an attractive option to arguing that it should become standard practice.

331   PRINGLE MLK (ed)(1967) *Adoption: facts and fallacies* Longman. 251pp.
Reviews of US, UK and European research in this field from 1948 to 1965.

332   SACHDEV P (ed)(1984) *Adoption: current issues and trends* Butterworth. 304pp.
Twenty papers on adoption in North America covering philosophy and concepts, process in adoption, dilemmas and the current scene and future outlook.

333   **SMITH CR (1984) *Adoption and fostering: why and how* Macmillan 165pp.
Practice guide derived from theoretical and research base and set in a UK social and legal context.

334   *SORICH CJ & SIEBERT R (1982) 'Towards humanizing adoption' *Child Welfare* 61,4,April, 207-216.
Account of one US agency's successful experiment with alternatives to closed adoption providing a continuum of openness: *sharing*, where photographs and other information are shared with the birth parents, perhaps every four months for the first five years; *semi-open*, where birth and adoptive parents meet but no information is exchanged; and *open*, where there is full sharing of identifying information.

335   SOROSKY AD, BARAN A & PANNOR R (1978) *The adoption triangle: the effects of the sealed record on adoptees, birth parents and adoptive parents* NY: Anchor Press. 256pp.
A study using questionnaire material from a self-selected group of respondents. The authors argue for greater openness in adoption in place of the current US 'sealed record' position.

336   TRISELIOTIS J & HILL M (1987) 'Children and adoption allowances' *Adoption & Fostering* 11,1, 35-39.
Pilot study of nine children aged nine and over whose adoptive parents are receiving an adoption allowance. Even for those previously fostered in the same home, the change to adoptive status was important. The idea of adoption allowances was largely accepted in a matter-of-fact way, and some children were strongly in favour of them. (See also 320.)

NATURAL/BIRTH PARENTS IN ADOPTION

From the evidence of the studies available, parents who give up their children for adoption are all too often left with unresolved feelings of loss and guilt, though the fact that those parents studied are usually either self-selected or drawn from 'clinical' populations raises some doubt as to how typical their experiences and reactions are. The study by SIMMS & SMITH suggests that teenage mothers who decide to keep their babies face tensions and difficulties of a different sort. As in foster family care and child welfare generally, birth parents in adoption seem to receive much less attention in the literature than do children or adoptive parents.

337   **BAAF (1986) *Child from the past* BAAF.
338   **BAAF (1987) *Single, pregnant and thinking about adoption* BAAF.
Basic information leaflets. The first is intended for birth parents who placed a child for adoption years ago and concentrates on the change in the law which gave adopted children the right to see their birth certificate at age 18. The second leaflet provides information about having a child adopted and includes a list of organisations offering advice and support for the single pregnant woman.

339   BARTH RP (1987) 'Adolescent mothers' beliefs about open adoption' *Social Casework* 68,6,June, 323-331.
Survey of school-age mothers considering adoption shows that they expected to wonder about their child in the future and that this uncertainty about the child's future had the most powerful influence on their decision. Author considers that more openness in adoption practice might free birth parents to make the decision most appropriate to their children's needs.

340   DEYKIN EY, CAMPBELL PHL & PATTI P (1984) 'The post-adoption experience of surrendering parents' *American Journal of Ortho-psychiatry* 54,2,April, 271-280.
Study shows that surrendering a child for adoption can have continuing negative effects on birth parents. Highlights the need for careful work with parents at the point of relinquishment.

341   MECH EV (1986) 'Pregnant adolescents: communicating the adoption option' *Child Welfare* 65,6,Nov/Dec, 555-567.
Study suggesting that pregnant adolescents would be interested in adoption for their children but counsellors have difficulty in presenting this as an option. Author argues that counsellors have a responsibility, given the characteristically limited ability of adolescents to plan ahead and to anticipate the consequences of a decision.

342   MILLEN L & ROLL S (1985) 'Solomon's mothers: a special case of pathological bereavement' *American Journal of Orthopsychiatry* 55,3,July, 411-418.
Study of 22 women undergoing psychotherapy who had earlier given up a child for adoption. Bereavement process when relinquishing child had been delayed or distorted.

343   PANNOR R, BARAN A & SOROSKY AD (1978) 'Birth parents who relinquished babies for adoption revisited' *Family Process* 17,3, Sept, 329-337.
Research study of 38 birth parents (a somewhat self-selected group): feelings of loss, pain and mourning continued to be felt years after relinquishment. Authors advocate more 'open' approach to adoption, allowing birth parents to update their knowledge of their relinquished children.

344   RAYNOR L (1971) *Giving up a baby for adoption* ABAA. 75pp.
Research study of the attitudes of mothers to the timing and finality of adoption consents (prior to the 1975 legislation on 'freeing').

345   RESNICK MD (1984) 'Studying adolescent mothers' decision making about adoption and parenting' *Social Work* 29,1,Jan/Feb, 5-10.
Discussion of US research findings, with proposals as to theoretical and methodological questions which might be considered in any future investigations.

346   SHAWYER J (1979) *Death by adoption* New Zealand: Cicada Press. 291pp.
"Adoption is a violent act, a political act of aggression towards a woman who has supposedly offended the sexual mores by committing the unforgivable act..." From the opening sentence, this is clearly an angry book, born of the author's experience as a single mother and the experience of other women similarly placed. Includes interviews with birth parents, adopted people, and a social worker equally disenchanted with the system.

347   SIMMS M & SMITH C (1982) 'Teenage mothers and adoption' *Adoption & Fostering* 6,4, 43-48.
Study undertaken in 1979 of a national sample of 533 teenage mothers in England and Wales at a point when their babies were about four months old. Interviewed about their lives, their babies and their partners, most felt that things had worked out better than expected, though money and uncertainties in relationships were clearly problems for some. Those who had considered adoption but rejected the idea were mostly satisfied with their decision but for others, trapped in poverty and unwanted domesticity, the outcome was proving less satisfactory.

348   WATSON KW (1986) 'Birth families: living with the adoption decision' *Public Welfare* 44,2,Spring, 5-10.
Discusses the impact of the adoption decision on various aspects of birth parents' lives, and some implications for agency policy and practice.

ADOPTIVE PARENTS

For insight into the nature of adoptive parenthood, KIRK's *Shared fate*, first published in 1964 and recently revised, has not been bettered. Similarly, ROWE remains, in this latest edition, the best primer for intending adopters and a helpful guide for others as well. People considering adoption need material which is positive but unsentimental, of which JONES and AUSTIN are excellent examples. On preparing and generally working with adopters, HARTMAN 1979 offers a clear, concise exposition of an approach based on a philosophy of sharing and learning together with the applicants, in contrast to 'inquisitorial' methods which elevate the social worker to the status of omniscient expert. HARTMAN 1984 uses the same principles in working with the adoptive family up to and beyond the making of the adoption order. Encouragement for advocates of single-parent adoption is to be found in the studies by DOUGHERTY, FEIGELMAN & SILVERMAN 1977, and KADUSHIN.

349   **AUSTIN J (ed)(1985) *Adoption: the inside story* Barn Owl Books. 180pp.

A collection of short articles on the 'problems, pains and pleasures' of adoptive family life by members of Parent to Parent Information on Adoption Services. The general tone is positive but there is no attempt to gloss over the pain and sheer hard work often involved.

350   **BAAF (1986) *Step-children and adoption (England and Wales)* BAAF.

351   **BAAF (1987) *Step-children and adoption (Scotland)* BAAF.

352   **BAAF (1985) *Talking about origins* BAAF.

Three information leaflets: the first and second addressed to parents and step-parents; and the third described as 'an open letter to adoptive parents' explaining the law on adopted children of 18 and their access to birth certificates.

353   *BAAF (1986) *Information for adoptive parents about their child's background* BAAF.

Practice note outlining the arguments for and against telling adoptive parents about a child's origins; the methods of disclosing the information; and basic principles guiding the selection of information and how it is presented.

354   BREBNER CM, SHARP JD & STONE FH (1985) *The role of infertility in adoption* BAAF. 75pp.

Material from a longitudinal study of infertile couples adopting, highlighting the impact of their infertility on the process.

355   **CHENNELLS P (1987) *Explaining adoption to your adopted child: a guide for adoptive parents* 32pp. BAAF.

Informative booklet for adoptive parents on why telling children is important; what and when to tell; telling children of a different racial or national origin; the special concerns of disabled children; and tracing birth parents.

356   DOUGHERTY SA (1978) 'Single adoptive mothers and their children' *Social Work* 23,4,July, 311-314.

Postal questionnaire study of 82 single women who had adopted privately in Washington DC. Successful, educated women, they were aware of the need for community support but sought this informally rather than through official sources. Showed same kinds of motivation as married couples.

357   **EVANS MS (1986) *"You don't have to fill in a form to have a baby": the frustrations and fulfilment of the adoption process* Family Welfare Association. 44pp.

Account of a couple's experiences from the point at which they had to face their childlessness to their becoming adoptive parents.

358   *FEIGELMAN W & SILVERMAN AR (1977) 'Single parent adoptions' *Social Casework* 58,7,July, 418-425.
Study shows that single parent applicants (especially men) are much more likely to encounter resistance from adoption agencies and disapproval from their friends than do married couples, but that adoption outcomes do not justify these negative expectations.

359   *FEIGELMAN W & SILVERMAN AR (1983) *Chosen children: new patterns of adoptive relationships* NY: Praeger. 261pp.
Study of 'preferential' adopters (adopting for social/humanitarian reasons rather than because of infertility) shows them to be more willing than traditional adopters to consider hard-to-place children, and successful when they do; more open in communication about adoption with their children than are traditional adopters.

360   FEIGELMAN W & SILVERMAN AR (1986) 'Adoptive parents, adoptees and the sealed record controversy' *Social Casework* 67,4, 219-226.
US study found a large sample of adoptive parents more receptive to the idea of opening adoption records than previous research has suggested.

361   **HARTMAN A (1979) *Finding families: an ecological approach to family assessment in adoption* California: Sage Foundation. 107pp.
Beginning with a brief history and account of the assumptions underlying 'old' and 'new' approaches to the selection of adopters, the author provides a clear and detailed exposition of the 'ecological' approach, which seeks to involve the applicants as partners in the process and to take account of their wider social environment. Detailed guidance on the use of the ecomap, geneogram, and sculpting techniques.

362   *HARTMAN A (1984) *Working with adoptive families beyond placement* NY: Child Welfare League of America. 61pp.
Might be regarded as a sequel to HARTMAN 1979, applying ecological principles to work with adoptive families post-placement and, as appropriate, post-adoption.

363   HOUGHTON D & HOUGHTON P (1984) *Coping with childlessness* Allen & Unwin. 176pp.
Drawing on evidence from the National Association for the Childless the authors seek to demonstrate the sense of stigma still experienced by people who are involuntarily childless. They argue for better facilities for the treatment of infertility as well as for greater understanding.

364   HUMPHREY M (1969) *The hostage seekers: a study of childless and adopting couples* Longmans. 162pp.
Classic study, still well worth reading for its vivid accounts of the social and personal implications of childlessness.

365   HUMPHREY M & KIRKWOOD R (1982) 'Marital relationship among adopters' *Adoption & Fostering* 6,2, 44-48.
Follow-up study of 17 adoptive couples matched with natural parent couples. Natural mothers gave more indication of marital dissatisfaction. The adoptive parents were more satisfied with their lot – more content with the drastically reduced social life; adoptive mothers less concerned to seek outside employment; took greater pride in their homes. Emphasis on sharing but otherwise wholly conventional in their approach to married life.

366   **JONES M (1987) *Everything you need to know about adoption* Sheldon Press. 98pp.
Clear straightforward information for prospective adopters on the issues and practicalities of present-day adoption. Excellent introduction.

367   KADUSHIN A (1970) 'Single-parent adoptions: an overview and some relevant research' *Social Service Review* 44,3,Sept, 263-274.
A review of research indicates that the single-parent family is merely a different forum for child-rearing and not inherently or necessarily harmful to children.

368   **KIRK HD (1984) *Shared fate: a theory and method of adoptive relationships* Washington: Ben-Simon Publications. 202pp.
Classic demonstration of the idea that there is nothing so practical as a good theory, providing keen insights into the dilemmas of adoptive parenthood, and stressing the importance of acknowledging rather than rejecting the differences from 'natural' parenthood.

369   MACKIE AJ (1982) 'Families of adopted adolescents' *Journal of Adolescence* 5, 167-178.
Writer argues that the crisis around issues of loss and sexuality which parents ordinarily face when their children reach adolecence is intensified for adoptive parents because of their infertility. Suggests incestuous feelings may be harder to handle than for natural parents. Makes the point that it is adoptive parents rather than their children who have to cope with the burden of being specially chosen.

370   PICTON C (1977) 'Post-adoption support' *Adoption & Fostering* 1,2, 21-25.
Argues the case for post-adoption services, particularly in view of the changing nature of adoption itself.

371   **ROWE J (1982) *Yours by choice: a guide for adoptive parents* Routledge & Kegan Paul. 188pp
Everything you would have liked to ask while they were assessing you...! Though intended for adoptive parents, it may usefully be read by anyone interested in adoption.

372 SENZEL B & YEAKEL M (1970) 'Relationship capacity and "acknowledgment-of-difference" in adoptive parenthood' *Smith College Studies in Social Work* 40,2, 155-163.
Small-scale but interesting study seeking to test Kirk's theory of adoptive relations in practice.

373 SHAPIRO CH & SEEBER BC (1983) 'Sex education and the adoptive family' *Social Work* 28,4,July/Aug, 291-296.
The authors argue that adoptive families face unique challenges in sex education, and identify ways in which social workers may facilitate family communication on sex-related topics.

374 WARD M (1978) 'Large adoptive families: a special resource' *Social Casework* 59,7,July, 411-418.
A large family may be the most appropriate adoptive home for children who have relationship difficulties, or who have particular needs for socialisation, structure or cultural enrichment.

375 WIEHE VR (1976) 'Attitudinal change as a function of the adoptive study' *Smith College Studies in Social Work* 46,2,March, 127-136.
Research suggesting that the 'adoptive study' does change applicants' attitudes in relation to unmarried parents and to telling children about adoption. Change on the question of the adopters' infertility was in a negative direction, perhaps because of being given insufficient attention. Both individual and group methods produced change.

376 WOLF PA & MAST E (1987) 'Counseling issues in adoptions by stepparents' *Social Work* 32,1,Jan/Feb, 69-74.
Study undertaken in Pennsylvania where step-parent adoptions now outnumber non-relative adoptions. Regarded by the families as positive, non-problematic family business. They seldom request counselling but tend to regard it as intrusive. Main reasons for adopting: name change; family unity/stability; child's good relationship with step-parent; transfer of legal rights to step-parent; wish to deny or sever relationship with other birth parent.

ADOPTED CHILDREN

The welcome decline in the number of studies anxiously seeking to determine how 'successful' adoptions are seems to date from the time when the National Child Development Study began to show that, in most respects, children who are adopted turn out at least as well as children in other situations (SEGLOW *et al*, BAGLEY, LAMBERT). A review of the literature on 'growing up adopted' is to be found in BEAN (313).

377   ANSFIELD JG (1971) *The adopted child* Springfield, Illinois: Charles C Thomas. 56pp.
Anecdotal "leaves from a psychiatrist's casebook" approach produces an inevitably gloomy view of adoption, adolescence and life in general. Main message is the author's belief that most adopted children would be better off not knowing the truth about their origins or, if they do have to find out, the later the better.

378   **BAAF (1986) *If you are adopted* BAAF.
Pace ANSFIELD (above), this leaflet is addressed to young people who have been adopted, offering answers to some common questions and information on tracing birth parents.

379   BACHRACH CA (1983) 'Children in families: characteristics of biological, step-, and adopted children' *Journal of Marriage & the Family* Feb, 171-179.
Demographic study of children living with biological, step- and adoptive mothers, found the adopted children to be better off economically than the others.

380   BAGLEY C (1980) 'Adjustment, achievement and social circumstances of adopted children in a national survey' *Adoption & Fostering* 4, 4, 47-49.
Independent analysis of the data from the National Child Development Study. (See also 006, 394 and 397.)

381   BELLUCCI MT (1975) 'Treatment of latency-age adopted children and parents' *Social Casework* 56, 5, May, 297-301.
Account of an Ohio agency's group therapy programme for children aged 9-13 years newly placed for adoption, each of whom had experienced at least five foster home changes. Discusses themes emerging in the sessions, including the children's anger. Parallel group for the adoptive parents.

382   BOHMAN M (1970) *Adopted children and their families: a follow-up study of adopted children, their background, environment and adjustment* Stockholm: Proprius. 239pp.
Swedish study suggesting that children's adjustment in adoption is relatively independent of such background variables as circumstances of pregnancy or birth, social class, age at placement, &c. Over-representation of behaviour disturbances in adopted boys may be connected more to the adoptive situation and the attitudes of the adoptive parents to their former childlessness.

383   BOHMAN M & SIGVARDSSON S (1980) 'Negative social heritage'
Adoption & Fostering 4, 3, 25-31.
Studies show a positive outcome for boys adopted from parental backgrounds
which include alcoholism or criminality.

384   *BRODZINSKY DM (1984) 'New perspectives on adoption revelation'
Adoption & Fostering 8, 2, 27-32 & 26.
Telling children about their adoption needs to be related to their level of cognitive
understanding. Young children may learn the words but not the ideas, and
information has to be updated through childhood.

385   *BRODZINSKY DM, SINGER LM & BRAFF AM (1984) 'Children's
understanding of adoption' *Child Development* 55, 3, June, 869-878.
Interviews with 200 adopted and non-adopted children aged 4-13 years about their
understanding of adoption. Results indicated clear developmental trends in
children's knowledge of the nature of the adoptive family relationship. Relatively
few differences were found, however, between adopted and non-adopted children's
knowledge of adoption. (See also 398.)

386   BRODZINSKY DM, SCHECHTER DE, BRAFF AM & SINGER
LM (1984) 'Psychological and academic adjustment in adopted children'
Journal of Consulting & Clinical Psychology 52, 4, 582-590.
Study in which boys and girls were found to be rated (by their mothers and teachers)
as higher in psychological and school-related behaviour problems and lower in
social competence and school achievement than were non-adopted children.
However, the differences were marginal and the behaviours still within the normal
range.

387   CAREY WB, LIPTON WL & MYERS RA (1974) 'Temperament in
adopted and foster babies' *Child Welfare* 53, 6, June, 352-358.
Pennsylvania study of 66 mothers and their infants suggested that stress in
pregnancy has no lasting effects on babies. Any apparent effects may be attributable
to the continued distress of a mother caring for her baby after delivery.

388   *CLARKE AM (1981) 'Adoption studies and human development'
Adoption & Fostering 5, 2, 17-29.
Review of various research studies on adoption outcome in relation to intelligence,
emotional adjustment and achievement.

389   FARBER S (1977) 'Sex differences in the expression of adoption
ideas: observations of adoptees from birth through latency' *American
Journal of Orthopsychiatry* 47, 4, Oct, 639-650.
Small study suggesting that girls manifest greater interest as well as conflict in
relation to adoption than do boys, and that interest and conflict are greatest for both
sexes during the latency period (though few children in this study had reached
adolescence).

390   FINCH R & JAQUES P (1985) 'Use of the geneogram with adoptive families' *Adoption & Fostering* 9, 3, 35-41.
Article drawing on work with adopted children referred to child guidance clinic. Practice illustrations.

391   HARDY-BROWN K, PLOMIN R, GREENHALGH J & JAX K (1980) 'Selective placement of adopted children: prevalence and effects' *Journal of Child Psychology & Psychiatry* 21, 143-152.
'Selective placement' refers to the attempt to match characteristics of birth parents (or child) and adoptive parents. Paper seeks to establish the extent to which selective placement is practised and its effects. Research suggests that such matching would make no difference to adopted children's cognitive development. The authors argue that, in relation to behavioural characteristics, agencies might do well to consider *negative* matching, ie placing children from the least favourable backgrounds with the most promising adopters.

392   KRAUS J (1978) 'Family structure as a factor in the adjustment of adopted children' *British Journal of Social Work*, 3, Autumn, 327-337.
Australian study of different patterns found in adoption concludes that the proportion of boys with serious behaviour dysfunction is ten times greater in families comprising the adopted child and a child born after the adoption than in families comprising only two or more adopted children.

393   KREMENTZ J (1982) *How it feels to be adopted* Gollancz. 108pp.
Accounts by 19 American children aged 8-16 years.

394   LAMBERT L (1981) 'Adopted from care by the age of seven' *Adoption & Fostering* 5, 3, 28-36.
Analysis of the circumstances of children in the National Child Development Study who were adopted from care. (See also 006, 380 and 397.)

395   MUNSINGER H (1975) 'The adopted child's IQ: a critical review' *Psychological Bulletin* 82, 5, Sept, 623-659.
Technical article reviewing research in this area, and concluding that heredity is much more important than environment in producing differences in IQ.

396   PROCH K (1982) 'Differences between foster care and adoption: perceptions of adopted foster children and adoptive foster parents'. *Child Welfare* 61, 5, May, 259-268.
Illinois study consisting of interviews with 56 sets of adoptive foster parents and 29 adopted foster children who would be regarded as hard to place. Explores foster parents' reasons for adopting and their own and the children's perceptions of the change of status.

397   SEGLOW J, PRINGLE MK & WEDGE P (1972) *Growing up adopted: a long-term national study of adopted children and their families* National Foundation for Educational Research. 200pp.
First major report on the National Child Development Study in relation to adopted children, indicating that they were doing every bit as well as children in other kinds of family setting. (See also 006, 380 and 394.)

398   SINGER LM, BRODZINSKY DM & BRAFF AM (1982) 'Children's beliefs about adoption: a developmental study' *Journal of Applied Developmental Psychology* 3, 285-294.
Study suggesting that, during early childhood, non-adopted children have a more negative view of adoption than do adopted children; by age 10-11, there are no significant differences; with increasing age, non-adopted children become less negative, adopted children rather more negative. (See also 385.)

399   STEIN LM & HOOPES JL (1985) *Identity formation in the adopted adolescent: the Delaware Family Study* NY: Child Welfare League of America. 83pp.
Study of 50 adopted and 41 non-adopted white adolescents indicates that the former do not display significantly more psychological problems than the latter. Highlights the importance of the quality of family relationships and openness in communication. Of those adopted, the minority interested in seeking their natural parents were slightly less well adjusted and included those who perceived their family relationships as most unsatisfactory.

400   *TRISELIOTIS JP & RUSSELL J (1984) *Hard to place: the outcome of adoption and residential care* Heinemann. 228pp.
Scottish comparative study of two groups of young adults: one group consisted of children who had been adopted from care between the ages of two and ten; while the other group was of children who had come into care below the age of ten and remained there at least until the age of 18. A much higher proportion of the adopted group (over 80%) rated their experiences of growing up positively than did the residential group (55%). An interesting point to emerge was that residential staff seemed to have as much difficulty as the adoptive parents in discussing the children's origins.

401   *WEISS A (1984) 'Parent-child relationships of adopted adolescents in a psychiatric hospital' *Adolescence* 19, 73, Spring, 77-88.
Study showing that adopted adolescents were hospitalised more often than non-adopted adolescents for less serious problems. Adoptive parents were mentioned more often than non-adoptive parents as being involved in the problems precipitating hospitalisation; and their visits were more restricted by the psychiatrists. Adoptive parents were also referred more often than non-adoptive parents for parallel group treatment.

402 *WILSON MR, GREENE JH & SOTH NB (1986) 'Psychodynamics of the adopted patient' *Adoption & Fostering* 10, 1, 41-46.
Study of adopted adolescents referred for psychiatric hospital treatment in Minnesota indicates three main areas of concern: rejectability; 'independence' (meaning an early pattern of self-reliance and inability to depend on others); and rootlessness.

ADOPTION OF CHILDREN WHO ARE 'HARD TO PLACE'

As was mentioned at the start of the ADOPTION section, this has been the growth area in writing and practice in recent years. In contrast to the 1940s, '50s and early '60s, when agencies had their elaborate (if often dubious) criteria of eligibility and suitability for children they were prepared to accept, the rule-books have been radically revised, or abandoned, to meet the challenge of the slogan 'no child is unadoptable'. The slogan was employed as the title for a collection of papers edited by CHURCHILL *et al* which makes as good an introduction as any to this area of policy and practice. It is to be hoped, incidentally, that social workers have firmly committed to memory the knowledge and skills needed to place healthy, white babies, as these are rapidly disappearing from the literature, though not from adoption agency lists!

Older children

Of all the factors making children hard to place, age probably remains the greatest obstacle in practice. The review of research by GOLDHABER & COLMAN introduced a note of caution to temper earlier enthusiasm, and writers such as GILL, KATZ and WARD have never sought to minimise the difficulties encountered when placing in new families children who are old enough to have a sense of their own past. The most recent and most alarming study in this respect is that by REID *et al*. More encouragement for older-child adoption is to be found in KERRANE *et al*. For those interested in practice issues, JEWETT is the obvious recommendation. Several of the papers in SAWBRIDGE (446) are also relevant to older children.

403 **ASTON E (1981) *Getting to know you* BAAF. 44pp.
Booklet intended to promote discussion of the difficulties which parents and older children (adopted or fostered) face in getting to know one another.

404 **BAAF (1987) *Meeting children's needs through adoption and fostering* BAAF.
Pamphlet addressed to people wondering about adopting an older or handicapped child or becoming a foster parent.

405 BORGMAN R (1982) 'The consequences of open and closed adoption for older children' *Child Welfare* 61, 4, Apr, 217-226.
Writer argues that open adoption is appropriate for older children, who have a need for continuity as well as permanency.

406 **CHURCHILL SR, CARLSON B & NYBELL L (eds) (1979) *No child is unadoptable: a reader on adoption of children with special needs* California: Sage Publications. 173pp.
Useful collection of papers (previously scattered through various US journals) looking at changing concepts of 'the adoptable child' and 'the adoptive family', and practice methods with 'special needs' children. Mainly on older children but some attention to black children and to children with medical conditions.

407 CORDELL AS, NATHAN C & KRYMOW VL (1985) 'Group counselling for children adopted at older ages' *Child Welfare* 64, 2, Mar/April, 113-124.
Account of a project providing a support group for older adopted children and others being prepared for adoption.

408 DERDEYN AP (1979) 'Adoption and the ownership of children' *Child Psychiatry & Human Development* 9, 4, summer, 215-226.
The changing focus of adoption from babies to older children with a sense of their past raises questions about the traditional secretiveness of adoption practices, given the importance of continuity in children's development.

409 DONLEY K (1975) *Opening new doors: finding families for older and handicapped children* ABAA. 56pp.
Edited version of talks given on this subject by Kay Donley, including her celebrated Ten Commandments.

410 *ELBOW M (1986) 'From caregiving to parenting: family formation with adopted older children' *Social Work* 31, 5, Sept/Oct, 366-370.
Discusses the three unique transitional tasks facing families who adopt older children – establishing boundaries, resolving losses and affirming roles – and their implications for social work practice.

411 FRATTER J, NEWTON D & SHINEGOLD D (1982) *Cambridge Cottage Pre-Fostering and Adoption Unit* Barnardo Social Work Paper 16. 83pp.
Account of the work of the unit, preparing children for family placement.

412   GILL MM (1978) 'Adoption of older children: the problems faced' *Social Casework* 59, 5, May, 272-278.
Group programme for families adopting older children encouraged expression of common post-placement concerns and provided strong support in problematic situations.

413   *GOLDHABER D & COLMAN M (1978) Review article on research into the adoption of older children *Adoption & Fostering* 2, 4, 41-48.
Takes a positive view generally but warns against a tendency in some retrospective studies to exaggerate the benefits of adoptive family life by devaluing the quality of the child's heritage.

414   **JEWETT CL (1978) *Adopting the older child* Mass: Harvard Common Press. 308pp.
Offers practitioners a wealth of material and ideas about adopting older children, conveyed through a series of case-examples.

415   **JEWETT CL (1982) *For ever and ever* BAAF. 28pp.
Booklet written primarily for adoptive parents of older children.

416   JONES ML (1979) 'Preparing the school-age child for adoption' *Child Welfare* 58, 1, Jan, 27-34.
Discussion of theoretical issues to be considered, using Kubler-Ross's framework of grief work.

417   KADUSHIN A (1970) *Adopting older children* NY: Columbia University Press. 245pp.
One of the earliest research studies to give encouragement to the idea of older child adoption. Interviews with 91 sets of adoptive parents whose children were aged five or older at placement. High level of parental satisfaction reported.

418   *KAGAN RM & REID WJ (1986) 'Critical factors in the adoption of emotionally disturbed youths' *Child Welfare* 65, 1, Jan/Feb, 63-73.
Albany (NY) study of 78 young people – mainly boys, all neglected and many physically abused – placed for adoption 1974-1982. An important success factor was the confidence of adoptive parents that they would not follow through on their destructive impulses towards the boys. Humour and creative discipline on the part of adoptive fathers also important. (See also 424.)

419   KATZ L (1977) 'Older child adoptive placement: a time of family crisis' *Child Welfare* 56, 3, March, 165-171.
The family crisis that inevitably follows adoptive placement of an older child can be overcome with the help of techniques based on crisis theory and family systems theory.

420   *KATZ L (1986) 'Parental stress and factors for success in older-child adoption' *Child Welfare* 65, 6, Nov/Dec, 569-578.
Author suggests as success factors adopters' tolerance of their own ambivalent feelings; refusal to be rejected by the child; ability to delay own gratification and to find happiness in small increments of improvement; role flexibility; a firm sense of entitlement; 'intrusive' and controlling qualities, exercised in a caring way; humour and self-care; and an open rather than closed family system.

421   *KERRANE A, HUNTER A & LANE M (1980) *Adopting older and handicapped children: a consumers' view of the preparation, assessment, placement and post-placement support services* Barnardo Social Work Paper 14. 139pp.
Consumer study of the New Families Project, Glasgow.

422   KNIGHT MR (1985) 'Termination visits in closed adoptions' *Child Welfare* 64, 1, Jan/Feb, 37-45.
On helping older children and their birth parents to say goodbye prior to adoption.

423   NIX H (1983) 'Sibling relationships in older child adoptions' *Adoption & Fostering* 7, 2, 22-28.
Theoretical and personal account of the issues involved in integrating an older adopted child into a family, urging greater attention to the sibling dimension.

424   *REID WJ, KAGAN RM, KAMINSKY A & HELMER K (1987) 'Adoptions of older institutionalized youth' *Social Casework* 68, 3, Mar, 140-149.
In this study – a sequel to KAGAN & REID (418) – the adoptions may be regarded as quite successful on the whole but at least half the adoptive parents were having to contend with serious and increasing problems and were experiencing disappointment, frustration and anxiety. The authors express their concern that the reversibility hypothesis advanced by Kadushin and others may not hold true after a certain adoptive age, or after the abuse, neglect, multiple placements and multiple losses experienced by the children in the present study. They suggest that 'professional' parenting may be more appropriate than adoption as a means of providing permanence for older disturbed children.

425   RUSHTON A & TRESEDER J (1986) 'Developmental recovery' *Adoption & Fostering* 10 ,3 , 54-57.
Brief review of studies by KADUSHIN (417), LAMBERT (394), Tizard & Hodges, THOBURN *et al* (092) and TRISELIOTIS & RUSSELL (400) of older children placed in permanent adoptive or foster homes; followed by an outline of the authors' own current research in the same area of study.

426   SMITH CL & PRICE E (1980) *Barnardo's New Families Project, Glasgow: the first two years* Barnardo Social Work Paper 13. 64pp.
Progress report on the early stages of a project to find homes for 'hard-to-place' children in care.

427   TIZARD B (1977) *Adoption: a second chance* Open Books. 251pp.
Study of five groups of children with the common factor of having experienced institutional care early in life: an 'early adopted' group, an 'early restored' group; a 'later adopted' and a 'later restored' group; and a 'fostered' group. Those adopted were the most fortunate – more stable situations, fewer emotional problems, and intellectually and academically 'superior' to the other groups.

428   TRISELIOTIS J (1985) 'Adoption with contact' *Adoption & Fostering* 9, 4, 19-24.
Reviewing issues relevant to access and contact, the author argues for the acceptance of continued contact with the birth family in older-child adoptions.

429   WARD M (1979) 'The relationship between parents and caseworker in adoption' *Social Casework* 60, 2, Feb, 96-103.
NB 'parent' here refers to adoptive not birth parent. Author discusses aspects of post-placement work, including the development of the adopters' sense of entitlement, with particular attention to older-child adoptions.

430   *WARD M (1981) 'Parental bonding in older child adoptions' *Child Welfare* 60, 1, Jan, 24-34.
Examines factors in the attachment process and shows major parallels between biological and older-adoptive parenting. Helpful discussion on the development of a sense of entitlement; validation of adoptive parenthood by societal support; ritual and 'claiming' behaviours; and the positive value of crises in developing mutual attachment.

Children with medical conditions and handicaps

WEDGE & THOBURN provide a good introduction to the field, reviewing the issues and some recent projects. The collection of papers by SAWBRIDGE and her colleagues, drawn from their experience with the pioneer agency, *Parents for Children*, is self-recommending for practitioners as is ARGENT for a more general readership. MACASKILL is concerned with the perspective of families who have adopted children with mental handicaps. The last of the series of articles by KNIGHT relates to a matter which is otherwise largely neglected, adoption applications from people who themselves have handicaps. The collection of short articles on medical conditions, edited by CURTIS (292), should also be noted.

431 **ARGENT H (1984) *Find me a family: the story of Parents for Children* Souvenir Press. 205pp.
"An attempt to describe how it feels to the children, the parents and the workers who become involved in special adoption".

432 COYNE A & BROWN ME (1985) 'Developmentally disabled children can be adopted' *Child Welfare* 64, 6, Nov/Dec, 607-615.
North American study offers encouraging findings on the possibility of adoption for children with mental and physical handicaps. Younger children (under eight years) did best, as did those adopted by foster parents. Rural agencies showed high level of success.

433 COYNE A & BROWNE ME (1986) 'Agency practices in successful adoption of developmentally disabled children' *Child Welfare* 65, 1, Jan/Feb, 45-52.
Study showing agency factors to be important, particularly decisiveness as expressed in specialisation, professionalisation, and centralisation of social work decision making.

434 FORSYTHE BJ & MARSHALL TW (1984) 'A group model for adoption studies for special-needs children' *Child Welfare* 63, 1, Jan/Feb, 56-61.
Texas comparative study with individual model showed group method to be more successful in achieving permanent placement and a more efficient use of staff time.

435 GLIDDEN LM (1985) 'Adopting mentally handicapped children: family characteristics' *Adoption & Fostering* 9, 3, 53-56.
Study of 42 families who had adopted or were fostering on a long-term basis children with mental handicaps. Demographic factors, motivation, and the adjustments of the families after placement were examined. Outcomes were very positive but the author argues the need for longitudinal research to trace developments over a longer period.

436 HOLLAND A & MURRAY R (1985) 'The genetics of schizophrenia and its implications' *Adoption & Fostering* 9, 2, 39-46.
Article followed by comments from Professor Sidney Brandon on the implications for the placement of children.

437 KNIGHT IG (1970) 'The handicapped child' *Child Adoption* 61, 3 of 1970, 33-38.

438 KNIGHT IG (1970) 'Placing the handicapped child for adoption' *Child Adoption* 62, 4 of 1970, 27-35.

439 KNIGHT IG (1971) 'Placement of children into families with a seriously handicapped child' *Child Adoption* 63, 1 of 1971, 56-59.

440   KNIGHT IG (1971) 'Applicants with severe handicaps' *Child Adoption* 64, 2 of 1971, 35-39.
Articles drawing on the writer's experience with Barnardo's at a time when children with handicaps were still generally thought to be unacceptable for adoption. The two 1971 papers are concerned with issues which even now receive little attention in the literature.

441   *MACASKILL C (1985) *Against the odds: adopting mentally handicapped children* BAAF. 100pp.
Detailed UK study of 20 adoptive families of children with mental handicaps. Interviews with social workers and families.

442   McINTURF JW (1986) 'Preparing special-needs children for adoption through use of a life book' *Child Welfare* 65, 4, July/Aug, 373-386.
Practical discussion on the use of life story books.

443   MORTON TD (1984) 'Training curriculum for workers in adoption of children with special needs' *Adoption & Fostering* 8, 2, 33-38.
Account of a US project to develop, field-test and disseminate a 45-hour in-service curriculum to train adoption workers in the placement of children with special needs. Article contains summaries of the content of each training session.

444   NELSON KA (1985) *On the frontier of adoption: a study of special-needs adoptive families* NY: Child Welfare League of America. 110pp.
US study of 257 adopted children over the age of eight, who have siblings and are moderately or severely impaired. High proportion (85%) of placements appear successful, though problems are not minimised – including the feeling of some families that they have been misled into taking a very difficult child.

445   OXTOBY M (ed) (1982) *Genetics in adoption and fostering: guidelines and resources* BAAF. 44pp.
Includes a paper by Professor CO Carter on genetics and adoption, and material produced by a BAAF medical group working party on genetic conditions and their implications for social workers in adoption, fostering and child care generally. (See also 329.)

446   **SAWBRIDGE P (ed) (1983) *Parents for children: twelve practice papers* BAAF. 88pp.
Collection of papers dealing with various aspects of placing 'hard-to-place' children: recruitment, selection and preparation of adopters; working with children and families in the placement process, and workshops for teenagers before placement.

447   SINCLAIR L (1985) 'Multiple placements of mentally handicapped children' *Adoption & Fostering* 9, 4, 37-40.
From experience with Barnardo's, the author argues the benefits of placing more than one child with a mental handicap in the same family.

448   **WEDGE P & THOBURN J (eds) (1986) *Finding families for 'hard-to-place' children: evidence from research* BAAF. 95pp.
Contributions by Diana Reich and Janet Lewis (on *Parents for Children*), Catherine Macaskill (on post-adoption support), and Stephen Wolkind (on children with medical and developmental problems). As well as setting the other contributions in context, the editors provide papers on family placement projects in Essex and Norfolk.

449   WOLKIND S (ed) (1979) *Medical aspects of adoption and foster care* Heinemann. 102pp.
Collection of papers dealing with issues such as handicap, child abuse, incest, and AID.

Sibling groups

As was mentioned in the corresponding section on FOSTER FAMILY CARE (299-302), the question of placing groups of brothers and sisters together or apart has only recently begun to receive the attention it merits.

450   JONES M & NIBLETT R (1985) 'To split or not to split: the placement of siblings' *Adoption & Fostering* 9, 2, 26-29.
Report of a workshop on the pros and cons of placing siblings in separate homes.

451   LePERE DW, DAVIS LE, COUVE J & McDONALD M (1986) *Large sibling groups: adoption experiences* Washington DC: Child Welfare League of America. 56pp.
Study of 190 sibling children placed with 52 families in Texas, with recommendations for placing large sibling groups.

452   WARD M (1987) 'Choosing adoptive families for large sibling groups' *Child Welfare* 66, 3, May/June, 259-268.
Author argues that social workers must look for particular parenting skills and resources in the adopting family, including administrative skills, community knowledge, the presence of adequate support systems and the ability to adapt.

Adults adopted as children

Must we call them 'adoptees', with its not so distant echo of 'amputee'? People who have been adopted are not easily accessible to researchers, unless referred to medical, psychiatric or social agencies, which helps to account for the pathological view of adoption put forward by many researchers. One group now receiving research attention are those seeking their original birth records, in some cases as a means of tracing their birth parents. HALL provides a helpful introduction to the background debate. While there is doubt as to how far this group may be considered representative of the great majority who do not seek out this information, they constitute a further source of insight into the adoption experience (TRISELIOTIS 1973 & 1983; PICTON; KOWAL & SCHILLING). Along with follow-up studies of agency placements, these studies indicate a largely positive view of their status by the people most centrally involved, though there are sometimes interesting differences in perception between those adopted and their adoptive parents (JAFFEE 1974, RAYNOR).

453   AUMEND SA & BARRETT MC (1983) 'Searching and non-searching adoptees' *Adoption & Fostering* 7, 2, 37-42.
454   AUMEND SA & BARRETT MC (1984) 'Self-concept and attitudes towards adoption: a comparison of searching and non-searching adult adoptees' *Child Welfare* 63, 3, May/June, 251-259.
Texas study shows substantial differences between adopted adults who do and those who do not seek out their birth parents.

455   AUTH PJ & ZARET S (1986) 'The search in adoption: a service and a process' *Social Casework* 67, 9, Nov, 560-568.
An adopted person's search for their birth parents is an emotionally charged issue for all members of the adoption triad. In this article, the search is treated as a professional casework service; and viewed as a developmental task and possible growth experience. Search may have various outcomes: a satisfying once-only meeting; a continuing relationship, but with the adoptive family remaining primary; a continuing relationship with the birth family becoming primary; an incomplete search; or rejection by the birth family.

456   ELDRED CA, ROSENTHAL D, WENDER PH, KETY SS, SCHULSINGER F, WELNER J & JACOBSEN B (1976) 'Some aspects of adoption in selected samples of adult adoptees' *American Journal of Orthopsychiatry* 46, 2, Apr, 279-290.
Danish research study raises doubts about some common assumptions regarding people who are adopted, especially as regards 'telling' and interest in origins.

457   *HAIMES E & TIMMS N (1985) *Adoption, identity and social policy: the search for distant relatives* Gower. 105pp.
Report of a DHSS-sponsored study to monitor the implementation of Section 26 of the Children Act 1975, which provided adopted people with access to their original birth records after 'compulsory counselling'. Particularly interesting for its consideration of the role and function of social workers in relation to compulsory counselling.

458   *HALL T (ed) (1980) *Access to birth records: the impact of section 26 of the Children Act 1975* BAAF. 36pp.
This useful pamphlet contains an introductory essay by Tony Hall and research studies by Alfred Leeding and Cyril Day on the operation of section 26, as well as appendices on the relevant legislation and procedures. (The paper by Day is also to be found in *Adoption & Fostering* 3, 4, 17-28; and a shorter version of Leeding's paper was published in the same journal, 1,3, 19-25.)

459   JAFFEE B & FANSHEL D (1970) *How they fared in adoption: a follow-up study* NY: Columbia University Press. 370pp.
Research based on interviews with the adoptive parents of 100 adopted young adults, with some interesting material on the notion of 'entitlement'. A major limitation of the study was its reliance on the perceptions of the adoptive parents only, although some amends are made in JAFFEE (1974), below.

460   JAFFEE B (1974) 'Adoption outcome: a two-generation view' *Child Welfare* 53, 4, April, 211-224.
Interviews with some of the young adopted adults whose adoptive parents' experiences were reported in JAFFEE & FANSHEL 1970, showing important differences in perception between the two groups, notably in the area of telling about adoption and having information about origins.

461   KOWAL KA & SCHILLING KM (1985) 'Adoption through the eyes of adult adoptees' *American Journal of Orthopsychiatry* 55, 3, July, 354-362.
Survey of 100 adopted people who contacted a social service agency or 'search' group regarding their adoption found that fantasising about birth parents is normal; more females than males initiate contact; and that the quest is for information rather than contact.

462 LINDSAY M & McGARRY K (1985) *Adoption counselling: a talking point* Dr Barnardo's Scottish Division. 79pp.
Account of the Scottish Adoption Advisory Service set up by Dr Barnardo's in 1978. Its increased use by birth parents, adoptive parents and people who have been adopted demonstrates the need for a comprehensive post-adoption service.

463 *PICTON C (1982) 'Adoptees in search of origins' *Adoption & Fostering* 6, 2, 49-52.
Australian study derived from interviews with members of Jigsaw, an association of adopted people, birth parents and adoptive parents. A consistent theme to emerge was of wanting to know about one's personal history and genealogy so as to complete one's sense of identity. The desire for knowledge was not linked to rejection of the adoptive parents.

464 *RAYNOR L (1980) *The adopted child comes of age* Allen & Unwin. 166pp.
Retrospective study of young adults placed as children by the Thomas Coram Foundation, based on case-records and interviews with the families.

465 STAFFORD G (1985) *Where to find adoption records: a guide for counsellors* BAAF. 83pp.
Useful collection of source material, addresses &c.

466 TOYNBEE P (1985) *Lost children: the story of adopted children searching for their mothers* Hutchinson. 199pp. Paperback edition published by Coronet in 1987. 242pp.
Journalistic account of various young people's experiences of 'searching'.

467 **TRISELIOTIS J (1973) *In search of origins: the experiences of adopted people* Routledge & Kegan Paul. 177pp.
Scottish study which helped the move to extend to English and Welsh adopted adults the right to obtain their original birth certificates.

468 *TRISELIOTIS J (1983) 'Identity and security in adoption and long-term fostering' *Adoption & Fostering* 7, 1, 22-31.
Research study suggesting that adopted children appear to develop a greater sense of security and identity than long-term foster children.

4 Ethnic issues in child welfare

GENERAL

Given the virtual absence of any consideration of gender in child welfare literature, it seems almost ungracious to complain of the limited treatment given to ethnic issues. However, there appears to be some kind of Iron Law operated by mainstream publishers and editors of books and journals on black issues: if it's child welfare, it must be adoption; if it's adoption, it must be transracial. The bibliography compiled from a wide range of sources by JOHNSON suggests the beginnings of a broader perspective. The papers edited by AHMED *et al* cover quite a variety of topics, though the omission of child abuse from any collection on 'working with families' in the mid-1980s is surprising. Of the other publications in this section, ROYS is the most substantial piece on the UK scene, and JENKINS & DIAMOND offer a thought-provoking study which might with profit be replicated here. The article by LOFTUS prompts the thought that children in black foster homes may well be getting a better deal than those in white foster homes, in terms of parental contact and chances of eventual restoration to their own families.

469   **AHMED S, CHEETHAM J & SMALL J (eds) (1986) *Social work with black children and their families* Batsford/BAAF. 207pp.
Papers on a range of issues including day care for the under-fives, black children in care, transracial placement, black self-concept, work with women and girls, and racist Intermediate Treatment.

470   BILLINGSLEY A & GIOVANNONI JM (1972) *Children of the storm: black children and American child welfare* NY: Harcourt Brace Jovanovich. 263pp.
US study which concludes that the child welfare system has failed black children. Discusses the effects of racism on the development of child welfare; efforts made to change the system; and changes still to be made.

471   *COOMBE V & LITTLE A (eds) (1986) *Race and social work: a guide to training* Tavistock. 233pp.
With sections on racism in society, ethnic minority communities, and social work responses and practice, this collection of short articles and exercises is intended as an in-service training guide for local authorities and voluntary agencies.

472   FIRST KEY (1987) *A study of black young people leaving care* London: First Key. 15pp.
Short but useful account of a study undertaken over an 18-month period (1984-5) in three London boroughs. Discusses the admission of young black people into the care system, the dangers of loss of identity while in care, and the needs of black young people leaving care.

473   GIBSON A (1986) *Westindian children in care or on the child abuse register* London: Centre for Caribbean Studies. 21pp.
Writing from his experience in Lambeth and Hackney, the author argues that Westindian (sic) children are placed on child abuse registers or admitted to care unnecessarily, because social workers fail to understand or appreciate parents' child-rearing attitudes and practices.

474   *JENKINS S & DIAMOND B (1985) 'Ethnicity and foster care: census data as predictors of placement variables' *American Journal of Orthopsychiatry* 55, 2, April, 267-276.
Epidemiological study showing the median time in care for black children to be 32 months compared with 20 months for white children. The researchers identified a 'large-city' factor – children living in large cities stay in care longer than children in the country as a whole – the difference being greater for white children. The fate of the white child coming into care in the city is more like that of the black child than of the white child elsewhere in the country. Black/white differences shrink with poverty – poverty integrates, and reduces the differences. Also where blacks are under-represented in an area, the chances of a black child being in care are twice as high as might be expected; where blacks are over-represented, black children are less likely to be in care.

475   JOHNSON MRD (1985) *Race and care: an indexed bibliography of material on multi-cultural welfare services.* University of Warwick Centre for Research in Ethnic Relations. 36pp.
Useful bibliography with introductory note but no annotations on individual items.

476   LOFTUS Y (1986) 'Black families and parental access' *Adoption & Fostering* 10, 4, 26-27.
Writing from her experience in a London borough homefinding unit, the author notes that black foster parents are often much more willing than white foster parents to maintain natural parent involvement and to work towards rehabilitation for the children.

477   RANDHAWA M (1985) 'Prevention and rehabilitation with black families' *Adoption & Fostering* 9, 3, 42-43.
Brief review of special features of work with black families.

478   *ROYS, P (1984) 'Ethnic minorities and the child welfare system' *International Journal of Social Psychiatry* 30, 1/2, Spring, 102-118.
Discussion of the structure and prevailing philosophy of the child welfare system in the UK, with particular reference to class and ethnic factors. While recognising the importance of the transracial placement issue, the writer warns against an over-concentration on that issue at the expense of wider questions about the relationship between black people and the child welfare system.

479   WALKER FC (1981) 'Cultural and ethnic issues in working with black families in the child welfare system' in PA SINANOGLU & AN MALUCCIO (eds) (see 208).
Writer discusses the particular situation of black families – economic and social pressures, kinship bonds, their strengths, the importance of religious factors – and argues that the child welfare system must make concerted efforts to understand cultural and ethnic issues. Of crucial importance is the use of informal helping systems within the community as well as the promotion of alternative community structures that provide intensive service to families.

FAMILY PLACEMENT

The volume of material on transracial placement – in effect, the placement of black children with white families – is such that it is not altogether easy to suggest a way in. Those with a special interest in the topic will plunge gratefully into the HARRIS bibliography. Others might start with the articles by CHESTANG and CHIMEZIE, which present the case against transracial placement powerfully and with passion. That there is passion on the other side of the argument also is clear from DALE's polemical pamphlet. Some researchers report that the children placed do as well as any (eg GROW & SHAPIRO; FEIGELMAN & SILVERMAN); but critics argue that such judgements are premature (the children studied had usually not yet reached adolescence), that researchers have been too reliant on the perceptions of adoptive parents, and that their research instruments are insensitive to such intangible but important issues as ethnic identity. McROY & ZURCHER and, in the UK, GILL & JACKSON, are mindful of these criticisms and more cautious in their conclusions. JOHNSON *et al* adopt the novel strategy of offering alternative conclusions from the same material.

Practitioners seeking positive ways out of the problems of transracial placement might usefully turn to the clear and thoughtful paper by BRUNTON & WELCH; the articles by SCHROEDER *et al* and by SMALL on finding black families; and MULLENDER & MILLER's account of a group intended to help children already in transracial placements. Incidentally, the term 'inracial' is coming into use amongst US writers to denote children adopted into families of similar race or ethnic background.

480   ABAFA (1977) *The Soul Kids Campaign: report of the steering group, London, 1975-1976'* ABAFA. 49pp.
Report of an early campaign to recruit black families for black children in care.

481   BAAF (1983) *Inter-country adoption: some basic guidelines for social workers* BAAF. 52pp.
Social, cultural, legal and procedural considerations.

483   **BRUNTON L & WELCH M (1983) 'White agency, black community' *Adoption & Fostering* 7, 2, 16-18.
Account of a recruiting campaign for black families in a London borough. Noteworthy in UK literature for its authors' recognition of institutionalised racism: for example, that problems in the recruitment of black families lie not in their reluctance to come forward but in agencies' reluctance to accept what is being offered.

484   **CHESTANG L (1972) 'The dilemma of biracial adoption' *Social Work* 17, 3, May, 100-105.
Opposed to transracial adoption on grounds of white families' inability to prepare black children to handle racism.

485   **CHIMEZIE A (1975) 'Transracial adoption of black children' *Social Work* 20, 4, July, 296-301.
Author argues the case against transracial adoption.

486   COMMISSION FOR RACIAL EQUALITY (1975) *Fostering black children* CRE. 36pp.
Discussion of issues, with recommendations.

487   DALE D (1987) *Denying homes to black children: Britain's new race adoption policies* Social Affairs Unit. 38pp.
Author claims that black children are being condemned to institutional care because of doctrinaire opposition to transracial family placement; and argues that such opposition stems from a 'spurious' political ideology rather than from any proper evaluation of the available research evidence.

488 *DAY D (1979) *The adoption of black children: counteracting institutional discrimination* Mass: Lexington Books. 156pp.
More a collection of papers than a book. Strong attack on racism in social work policy and practice. Particularly useful section on the interaction between white workers and black clients, and ways of breaking down the communication barriers.

489 FEIGELMAN W & SILVERMAN AR (1984) 'The long-term effects of transracial adoption' *Social Service Review* 58, 4, Dec, 588-602.
Follow-up after six years in placement finds no evidence to support critical attack on transracial adoption – children doing as well as their peers adopted inracially.

490 *GILL O & JACKSON B (1983) *Adoption and race: black, Asian and mixed race children in white families* Batsford/BAAF. 151pp.
Follow-up study of black children placed with white families by the British Adoption Project in the mid-1960s. Findings show that, on various indicators, the children have done well, but raise questions as to their sense of racial identity.

491 GROW LJ & SHAPIRO D (1974) *Black children, white parents: a study of transracial adoption* NY: Child Welfare League of America. 239pp.
Early US study of 125 transracially placed children concluded most were doing very well, but a substantial minority of families were 'in serious trouble'.

492 HARRIS K (1985) *Transracial adoption: a bibliography* BAAF. 122pp.
Annotated bibliography with 371 items from a wide range of UK and US sources. Invaluable reference for anyone with a special interest in this field.

493 HOWARD A, ROYSE DD & SKERL JA (1977) 'Transracial adoption: the black community perspective' *Social Work* 22, 3, May, 184-189.
US study suggesting that the majority of black people do not support the radicals' position against transracial adoption but favour such adoption when the alternative for children is to grow up in an institution.

494 JOHNSON PR, SHIREMAN JF & WATSON KW (1987) 'Transracial adoption and the development of black identity at age eight' *Child Welfare* 66, 1, Jan/Feb, 45-55.
Comparative study of transracial and black same-race adoptive placements by the Chicago Child Care Society and the Children's Home and Aid Society of Illinois between 1970 and 1972. Further studies are planned. Interesting feature of this paper is the presentation of alternative conclusions for and against transracial adoption derived from the same data, demonstrating that 'facts' never speak for themselves.

495   MADISON BQ & SCHAPIRO M (1973) 'Black adoption – issues and policies: review of the literature' *Social Service Review* 47, 4, Dec, 531-560.
Comprehensive review of issues and of adoption services for black children from 1945 to the early 70s.

496   McROY RG, ZURCHER LA, LAUDERDALE ML & ANDERSON RN (1982) 'Self-esteem and racial identity in transracial and inracial adoptees' *Social Work* 27, 6, Nov, 522-526.
Study suggesting transracially adopted children do not differ from children adopted inracially in self-esteem, but that there seems to be a difference in perception of racial identity.

497   McROY RG & ZURCHER LA (1983) *Transracial and inracial adoptees: the adolescent years* Springfield, Illinois: Charles C Thomas. 155pp.
Study of the experiences of black adolescents who were adopted very young transracially or inracially. According to the authors, this is the first study to examine both the adopted parents' and the young people's experiences. Employing symbolic interaction theory, the study looks broadly at their family and social environments.

498   McROY RG, ZURCHER LA, LAUDERDALE ML & ANDERSON RE (1984) 'The identity of transracial adoptees' *Social Casework* 65, 1, Jan, 34-39.
Research study suggests transracial adoption requires special efforts on the part of adoptive parents and children. Parents should be able realistically to perceive the child's racial identity to be different from their own.

499   MORIN RJ (1977) 'Black child, white parents: a beginning biography' *Child Welfare* 56, 9, Nov, 576-583.
Account by a white adoptive mother of her black adoptive child's struggle to develop his personal and social identity.

500   *MULLENDER A & MILLER D (1985) 'The Ebony Group: black children in foster homes' *Adoption & Fostering* 9, 1, 33-40 & 49.
Description of a group for black children placed with white foster families, intended to help the children deal with issues of race and racism. The authors accept the case for inracial placement but argue the need to help children already in transracial placements.

501   NATIONAL FOSTER CARE ASSOCIATION (undated) *I like you white. Do you like me black?* NFCA.
Leaflet for white families fostering black children.

502 *SCHROEDER H & LIGHTFOOT D (1983) 'Finding black families' *Adoption & Fostering* 7, 1, 18-21.

503 *SCHROEDER H, LIGHTFOOT D & REES S (1985) 'Black applicants to Ealing recruitment campaign' *Adoption & Fostering* 9, 2, 50-53.
Descriptive account of a project in a London borough to attract black foster and adoptive parents.

504 SHIREMAN JF (1970) 'Adoptive applicants who withdrew' *Social Service Review* 44, 3, Sept, 285-292.
Study of 80 predominantly black applicants to the Chicago Child Care Society seeking to adopt black children. Their withdrawal after initial contact raised questions about agency application procedures.

505 SHIREMAN JF & JOHNSON PR (1976) 'Single persons as adoptive parents' *Social Service Review* 50, 1, March, 103-116.
Four-year follow-up study of 18 single parent adoptions of black children in Chicago. Authors stress the need to sharpen up assessment skills so as to differentiate potentially strong and weak adoptive homes.

506 SHIREMAN JF & JOHNSON PR (1986) 'A longitudinal study of black adoptions: single parent, transracial, and traditional' *Social Work* 31, 3, May/June, 172-176.
Longitudinal study of 76 black children adopted in infancy (aged eight at the time of the study) showed most children in all categories doing well. In the transracial adoptions, the children's pattern of racial identity differed from those adopted inracially. Additional stresses were noted in the single-parent adoptions as well as the closeness of the parent-child relationship.

507 SILVERMAN AR & FEIGELMAN W (1981) 'The adjustment of black children adopted by white families' *Social Casework* 62, 9, Nov, 529-536.
Postal survey of 713 adoptive families produced findings supportive of transracial placement. Writers suggest apparent problems are related more to age than to race factors.

508 SIMON RJ & ALTSTEIN H (1977) *Transracial adoption* NY: Wiley. 197pp.

509   SIMON RJ & ALTSTEIN H (1982) *Transracial adoption: a follow-up* Lexington: Lexington Books. 148pp.
The first of these publications reports on a study of 204 families who had adopted transracially; the second is a follow-up of 133 of the families. Findings of the latter limited by being derived from a postal questionnaire addressed only to adoptive parents. The researchers hope to approach the children directly at a later stage. The books together provide a fascinating history of the rise and fall (and rise?) of transracial adoption in the US, concluding that transracial placement should be regarded as a resource but not a solution.

510   SMALL J (1982) 'New Black Families' *Adoption & Fostering* 6, 3, 35-39.
Account of the early progress of the New Black Families Unit, set up in Lambeth to find black families for black children.

511   SMALL JW (1984) 'The crisis in adoption' *International Journal of Social Psychiatry* 30, 1/2,Spring, 129-142.
Critical essay on transracial placement. Author also attacks use of term 'mixed race' and proposes 'mixed parentage' as a more acceptable alternative.

Author Index

First authors are shown in block capitals

Brown ME 1985   432
Brown ME 1986   433
BRUNTON L 1983   483
BRYANT B 1981   275
BRYER M 1988   066
Bufferd RK 1986   315
Bullock R 1985   204
Bullock R 1986   045
BUSH M 1977   259
BUSH M 1982   067, 122

Cain H 1984   178, 229
Campbell PHL 1984   340
CARBINO R 1980   213
Carey K 1986   054
CAREY WB 1974   387
Carlson B (ed) 1979   406
Carlson ML 1986   103
CATHOLIC CHILDREN'S SOCIETY
   1983   123
Cautley PW 1975   102
Cautley PW 1976   299
CAUTLEY PW 1980   214
CENTRAL COUNCIL FOR
   EDUCATION AND TRAINING IN
   SOCIAL WORK 1978   124
Chatterton SG 1983   326
Cheetham J (ed) 1986   469
CHENNELLS P 1987   355
CHESTANG L 1972   484
CHIMEZIE A 1975   485
CHURCHILL SR (ed) 1979   406
CLARK B 1977   068
Clark FW 1981   193
Clark GA (ed) 1977   138
CLARKE AM 1981   388
Cleaver H 1986   105
Cleaver H 1987   106
Colman M 1978   413
COLON F 1978   185
COMMISSION FOR RACIAL
   EQUALITY 1975   486
CONNOR T 1985   125
Cook T (ed) (1981)   148
COOMBE V (ed) 1986   471

COOPER J 1978   030
CORDELL AS (1985)   407
Couve J 1986   451
COYNE A 1985   432
COYNE A 1986   433
COX MJ (ed) 1985   153
Cox RD (ed) 1985   153
CRETNEY S 1984   186
CROMPTON M 1980   126
Cullen D 1986   025
CURTIS S (ed) 1987   292

DALE D 1987   487
DARE R 1984   237
DAVIDS L 1973   215
Davis LE 1986   451
DAVIS S 1984   238
DAY D 1979   488
DeBord MS 1984   190
DENTON G 1984   031
DEPARTMENT OF HEALTH AND
   SOCIAL SECURITY (DHSS)
   1976   154
DHSS 1983   187
DHSS 1985   032
Derbyshire M 1981   255
Derbyshire M 1982   256
DERDEYN AP 1979   408
Devis DA   318
DEVON CC SOCIAL SERVICES
   DEPARTMENT 1982   107
DEYKIN EY 1984
Diamond B 1985   474
DIMMOCK B 1985   144
DINNAGE R (ed) 1967   155
DIXON N 1987   293
Dodson L 1987   293
DONLEY K 1975   409
DONLEY K 1978   108
DONLEY K 1979   127
DOUGHERTY SA 1978   356
DOWNES C 1982   276, 277, 278
Dr Barnardo's – see BARNARDO'S
DUKETTE R 1984   316
Dunbar D 1985   125

HAMPSON RB 1980   219
Hardy J 1987   293
HARDY-BROWN K 1980   391
HARRIS K 1985   492
HART G 1987   296
HARTMAN A 1979   361
HARTMAN A 1984   362
Hartman A (ed) 1985   005
HARTMAN A 1987   036
Hawley D 1986   099, 100, 101
HAZEL N 1981   279
HEIM A 1983   319
Helmer K 1987   424
HESS P 1982   191
HESS PM 1986   192
HEYWOOD J 1978   001
HILL M 1986   320
Hill M 1987   336
Hipgrave T 1983   282
Hipgrave T 1985   159
HOGGETT B 1987   020
HOGGETT BM 1987   021
HOGHUGHI M 1985   159
HOKSBERGEN RAC (ed) 1986   321
HOLLAND A 1985   436
HOLMAN R 1973   060
HOLMAN R 1975   161
HOLMAN R 1980   002
Hoopes JL 1985   399
HOREJSI CR 1979   162
HOREJSI CR 1981   193
Hosie K 1985   204
Hosie K 1986   045
HOUGHTON D 1984   363
Houghton P 1984   363
HOWARD A 1977   493
Howard JA 1986   207
HOWE D 1987   322
HOWE GW 1983   075
HUGHES P 1984   194
HUMPHREY M 1969   364
HUMPHREY M 1982   365
Hundleby M 1984   178, 229
Hunter A 1980   421

HUSSELL C 1982   076

IRISH FOSTER CARE ASSOCIATION
   1984   163
ISAAC BC 1986   147

Jackson B 1983   490
JACOBS M 1980   244
Jacobsen B 1976   456
Jacques N 1986   047
JAFFEE B 1970   459
JAFFEE B 1974   460
JAFFEE ED 1979   037
Jaques P 1985   390
Jax K 1980   391
JENKINS S 1972   195
JENKINS S 1975   196
JENKINS S 1985   474
JEWETT CL 1978   414
JEWETT CL 1982   415
JEWETT CL 1984   132
JOHNSON D 1986   197
JOHNSON MRD 1985   475
Johnson PR 1976   505
Johnson PR 1986   506
JOHNSON PR 1987   494
JONES E 1986   220
JONES EO 1975   221
JONES M 1985   450
JONES M 1987   366
JONES MA 1976   038
JONES MA 1985   039
JONES ML 1979   416
JORDAN A 1984   245
JOSLING JF 1985   323

KADUSHIN A 1970   367, 417
KADUSHIN A 1971   003
KADUSHIN A 1974   077
KADUSHIN A 1977   004
KAGAN RM 1980   133
KAGAN RM 1986   418
Kagan RM 1987   424
Kaminsky A 1987   424
KATZ L 1977   419

McROY RG 1984   498
McWHINNIE AM 1979   247
MECH EV 1973   327
MECH EV 1985   203
MECH EV 1986   341
MEEZAN W 1982   223
MEEZAN W 1985   224
MEYER CH 1985   167
MILLEN L 1985   342
MILLER B 1986   225
Miller D 1985   500
MILLER J (ed) 1981   148
MILLHAM S 1985   204
MILLHAM S 1986   045
MILNER JL 1987   205
Minty EB 1986   147
MOLLAN C 1985   328
Monaghan B 1982   076
Moore LM 1984   175
MORIN RJ 1977   499
Morris B 1984   238
Morrison RM 1986   147
MORRISON T 1986   300
MORTON TD 1984   443
MULLENDER A 1985   500
MUNSINGER H 1975   395
Murcer B 1982   034
Murdoch A 1986   092
MURRAY L 1984   168
Murray R 1985   436
Myers RA 1974   387

NAPIER H 1972   169
Nathan C 1985   407
NATIONAL ASSOCIATION OF
   YOUNG PEOPLE IN CARE
   (NAYPIC) 1979   137
NAYPIC 1984   046
NATIONAL FOSTER CARE
   ASSOCIATION (NFCA)   226, 501
NFCA 1976   170
NFCA 1977   248
NFCA 1980   249
NFCA 1982   250

NFCA 1983   251
NFCA 1985   281
NFCA 1986   171
NFCA 1987   286, 298
NELSON KA 1985   444
Neuman R 1973   089
Neuman R 1976   038
Newton D 1982   411
Niblett R 1985   450
NIX H 1983   423
Norbury D 1983   326
Norman E 1972   195
Norman E 1975   196
Nybell L (ed) 1979   406

O'Brien A 1986   092
O'CONNELL M 1976   265
Olmstead KA 1986   081
OLSEN LJ 1982   082
Osborn AF 1987   050
Overstreet HMF 1972   164
OXTOBY M (ed) 1981   329
OXTOBY M (ed) 1982   445

PACKMAN J 1981   009
PACKMAN J 1986   047
PAGE R (ed) 1977   138
PANNOR R 1978   343
Pannor R 1978   335
PANNOR R 1983   330
PARDECK JT 1982   111
PARDECK JT 1987   139
Pardeck JA 1987   139
PARKER RA 1966   172
PARKER RA 1978   173
PARKER RA (ed) 1980   010
PARKER RA 1985   083
Parsloe P 1984   189
Patti P 1984   340
Pearl DS 1987   021
PENN JV 1978   252
Phillips D 1985   042
Phillips D 1986   033
PICTON C 1977   070
PICTON C 1982   463

Sherman A 1976   038
SHERMAN EA 1973   089
Shinegold D 1982   411
Shinn EB 1978   260
SHIREMAN JF 1970   504
SHIREMAN JF 1976   505
Shireman JF 1982   223
Shireman JF 1985   224
SHIREMAN JF 1986   506
Shireman JF 1987   494
Shyne AW 1973   089
Siebert R 1982   334
Sigvardsson S 1980   383
Silverman AR 1977   358
SILVERMAN AR 1981   507
Silverman AR 1983   359
Silverman AR 1984   489
Silverman AR 1986   360
Simmonds J (ed) 1987   117
SIMMS M 1982   347
SIMON RJ 1977   508
SIMON RJ 1982   509
Sinanoglu PA 1981   201
SINANOGLU PA (ed) 1981   208
SINCLAIR L 1985   447
SINCLAIR R 1984   053
SINGER LM 1982   398
Singer LM 1984   385, 386
Skerl JA 1977   493
SMALL J 1982   510
Small J (ed) 1986   469
SMALL JW 1984   511
Smith C 1982   347
SMITH CL 1980   426
SMITH CR 1984   333
SMITH G 1986   288
SMITH PM 1986   283
SOCIAL WORK SERVICE 1981   181
Solnit AJ 1973   073
Solnit AJ 1980   074
SOOTHILL K 1980   254
SOOTHILL K 1981   255
SOOTHILL K 1982   256
SORICH CJ 1982   334

Sorosky AD 1978   335
SOROSKY AD 1978   343
SOSIN MR 1987   090
Soth NB 1986   402
SOUTHON V 1986   026
Spencer C 1987   293
ST CLAIRE L 1987   050
STAFFORD G 1985   465
STEIN LM 1985   399
STEIN M 1983   055
STEIN M 1985   056
STEIN M 1986   054
STEIN TJ 1978   091
STEIN TJ 1983   057
STEIN TJ 1984   058
STEVENSON O 1977   232
Stone FH 1985   354
Streather J 1980   006
Surgent L 1976   240

Tavormina JB 1980   219
THOBURN J 1980   059
THOBURN J 1986   092
Thoburn J (ed) 1986   448
Thorn J 1984   238
Thorpe J 1975   146
THORPE R 1980   269
TIDDY SG 1986   209
TIMBERLAKE EM 1982   301
TIMBERLAKE EM 1987   284
Timms N 1985   457
TIZARD B 1977   427
Tolley ES 1986   087
TOYNBEE P 1985   466
TOZER R 1979   285
Tracy GS 1984   190
TRASLER G 1960   233
Treseder J 1986   425
TRISELIOTIS J 1973   467
TRISELIOTIS J 1980   070
TRISELIOTIS J (ed) 1980   182
TRISELIOTIS J 1983   468
TRISELIOTIS J 1985   428
Triseliotis J 1986   320

Title Index

Some titles have been abbreviated in the Index – see main entry for full titles

British Agencies for Adoption & Fostering

British Agencies for Adoption & Fostering (BAAF) is a registered charity and professional association for all those working in the child care field. BAAF's work includes:

providing training and consultation services to social workers and other professionals to help them improve the quality of medical, legal and social work services to children and families;

giving evidence to government committees on subjects concerning children and families;

responding to consultative documents on changes in legislation and regulations affecting children in or at risk of coming into care;

publishing a wide range of books, training packs and leaflets as well as a quarterly journal on adoption, fostering and child care issues;

giving advice and information to members of the public on aspects of adoption, fostering and child care issues;

and helping to find new families for children through the BAAF Exchange Service, 'Be My Parent' and 'Find a Family'.

More information about BAAF (including membership subscription details) can be obtained from BAAF, 11 Southwark Street, London SE1 1RQ.